THE BUSINESS OF HOTELS

9 Strategies to Build the Ultimate Hospitality Team

Guillaume Warnery

Published by

Business Growth Advisors

SYDNEY, AUSTRALIA

*An organized team can get
you through anything.*

— GUILLAUME WARNERY

MDA Publishing
Higginbotham Rd
Gladesville, NSW, 2111
Australia

Book Layout © 2021

The Business of Hotels -- 1st ed.
ISBN:978-0-6450942-5-1

Contacts

Linked In

linkedin.com/in/guillaumewarneryhospitalitycoachjordan/

Facebook

facebook.com/HOTELCOACH.PRO

Join our Facebook community

HOSPITALITY LEADERS TO GROW & PROFIT

www.facebook.com/groups/1389659848061265

What Industry leaders and clients have to say about THE BUSINESS OF HOTELS and working with Guillaume

When we met Guillaume, our business had reached the tipping point, exactly one year later the difference is as stark as night and day. The cost of hiring a coach? The past year has proven to be an investment in our future that we simply cannot place a value on.

Craig Corrie owner Events Unusual & Emma Corrie, Wedding & Event Designer - Barbados

Guillaume is a professional hotelier; exceptional entrepreneur, superior relationship extension skills and strong business acumen. Detail oriented, top line and bottom line results driven, focused on big picture. His international exposure working with a multi-cultural team managing upward and downward with ease. I truly enjoyed working with Guillaume.

Ken Helmy Hospitality Developer Entrepreneur - USA

I reported to Guillaume at Le Méridien New Orleans and he remains to this day one of the best manager I have been in contact with. His leadership skills, business acumen and empathy inspired me to become a better professional and person.

Jean Christophe Gazzo Fairmont - South Africa

Guillaume has a perfect attitude for hospitality industry. He always has the tendency to make people think and react to different situations and learn from it.

Saeed Shah Marriott – Canada

We collaborated with Guillaume during the pre-opening and running of our four-star lifestyle hotel in Beirut. It is a joy working with Guillaume, he is extremely generous with his time and knowledge, full of wisdom, humor and inspiration. He was particularly insightful during the recent and ongoing economic and political emergency in Lebanon, with his wealth of experience in hospitality, management and crisis control. For all his professional qualities, Guillaume remains exceptionally humble, easy to communicate with, always ready to listen and contribute with practical advice."

Christine Ozeir & Sebastian Kracun, co-owners of Bossa Nova Beirut Hotel - Lebanon

I worked with Guillaume in Islamabad Serena Hotel. He has that unflinching ability to adapt to the local conditions while understanding the people's behavior and their potential. This quality makes him a natural leader with positive and progressive attitude and we always considered him as one of us, helping us to discuss and make a number of progressive action-based strategies for business growth

Umer Raza Human Resources and Change management Lahore - Pakistan

Dear Guillaume, I want to express my gratitude for your support and priceless help on both my personal life and business growth. I always received practical and effective advises which I still put in practice.

Gianluca Trasatti, owner Café Gianluca at Timothy Olton Gallery - Barbados

It was an honor to work with a person of stature like Guillaume who had a wide experience in the

hospitality industry with an equally dynamic ad-
ministrative and managerial capabilities which is
a rare combination in itself. The close interaction
which I had with him, added a lot to my portfolio.

Naushad Noorani Financial Analyst, Dallas -
USA

Introduction

Every business that has ever taken their employees on a teambuilding experience can testify that teambuilding activities are great for a team's performance, communication, and morale. Building the right team takes time, patience and practice.

What better teambuilding experience can you have than preparing for an actual hurricane to hit your hotel. Preparing for this or any catastrophe for that matter, isn't an easy task. It takes incredible teamwork on the part of every hotel employee - from the manager to the restaurant staff to the housekeeping staff. With an organized and dedicated team, you can turn an otherwise disastrous event into a memorable (although scary) event that your guests will be talking about forever. So how was this done? In this book, I will share that and other personal experiences. I will show you how an organized team can get you through anything. I will share with you the makings of the perfect team.

Acknowledgements

I have greatly benefited from the wisdom and generosity of many people. I would specifically like to thank my family; specifically, my parents, my brothers, Marielle and Auguste. My gratitude also goes out to all of the General Managers I have worked with throughout my career in the hotel business; Thierry, Rudolf, Michael, Denis, Samir, Mark, Mario, Jean, Olivier, Jean Pierre and Khaled, and the many colleagues in the various hotels who will be too numerous to mention. They have all formed me as hotelier. I also thank my two coaches; Ian Blanchard in Barbados and Brett Odgers in Australia, as well as the benevolent support of the Million Authors Group and last but not least Hunny bunny, our editor extraordinaire. A special thanks to my wife, Violet, who allows me to do what I love to do.

About the Author

My name is Guillaume. I am French and Swiss, and raised in Africa and in many different parts of France. After high school, I studied at l'Ecole Hôtelière de Lausanne, Switzerland and immediately afterwards started my journey in Hotel industry. It gave me an amazing opportunity to work in many parts of the world from the Middle East, Africa, Asia, the Caribbean, and North, South & Central America. I have enjoyed discovering new cultures and working with diverse people from around the world while learning about different hotel operations.

After 25years in the hospitality industry, where my love of coaching and mentoring was evoked, I became a Business Coach with the Action COACH franchise in Barbados and in Lebanon from 2013-2020. With this book, I bring together my two passions for hotels and coaching into one venture. I hope to bring some of my enthusiasm, expertise and love to those who read this book or seek coaching support in the hotel industry.

My wife is working for UNICEF and we have two sons. Together we have moved around the world for more than 16 years now. After 6 years in Beirut, we moved recently to Amman in Jordan. When I am not coaching you can find me on the tennis court or the football field, and during weekend I like to explore the country of residence with family and friends.

I hope you will enjoy the book; it was a pleasure for me to write.

CONTENTS

Chapter One

WHY TEAMWORK IS THE ANSWER

We instructed our guests to pack their belongings and keep them in the bathtub (the safest place in the room) and place all their papers, passports, ID cards, cash and plane tickets in their room's safe. Their 5-star vacation on the pristine coastline of Cancun was about to change as Hurricane Emily was about to slam into the Yucatan Peninsula.

Cancun's last big evacuation was for Hurricane Gilbert in 1988, which killed some 300 people in Mexico and the Caribbean; however, the city and surrounding resort areas only had about 8,000 hotel rooms then. That number had since grown to over 50,000.

Storm preparations had also changed, improving with time. Back in the days of Gilbert, we didn't have prevention or prediction as I was told by our Jefe de Prevention (chief of Security). By the time we heard it was coming, it was already on top of us.

It was July 2005 and, as predicted, the powerful category 4* storm hit, bringing winds of nearly 135 mph. It knocked out power and phone service on Mexico's famous Riviera Maya coastline. Tourists were placed in shelters that had been set up in schools and hotel ballrooms. In Cancun, our hotel was authorized to transform the ballroom into a shelter for our guests and team members. That was good news as we didn't have to shut down, evacuate the hotel and move to a school inland only to transform that to a shelter, a far more complicated exercise.

* hurricane
A tropical cyclone with maximum sustained winds of 119 km/h (74 mph) or greater. The term "hurricane" is used for Northern Hemisphere tropical cyclones east of the International Dateline to the Greenwich Meridian. The term "typhoon" is used for Pacific tropical cyclones north of the equator, west of the International Dateline. Hurricanes are further designated by categories on the

Saffir-Simpson Scale. Hurricanes in categories 3, 4, 5 are known as "major" or "intense" hurricanes.

I was the executive manager of Le Meridien Cancun Resort & Spa and as per the process, my responsibility was to head the shelter and take charge of our team and client's safety.

The general manager and the heads of security and maintenance were in charge of the assets and the hotel. In case of evacuation of the hotel, they would stay and protect the building while other operational executive members – the executive chef, director of food & beverage, executive housekeeper, and I - would be with the leads in the shelter. A third group, the heads of human resources, IT and sales & marketing, would be on standby at their home and most likely be available to coordinate the aftermath.

The day before the expected storm, hundreds of buses moved more than 25,000 tourists to temporary shelters, only a portion of the 57,000 that were being evacuated from the entire region. Cancun's airport closed the day before the storm after thousands lined up at ticket counters, trying to get flights out before it hit. We tried to evacuate as many guests as possible, organizing the evacuation with the airlines up to the last flight leaving Cancun. Some of our guests were moved with buses to other parts of the Yucatan region.

Once the shelter was in place, guests were informed to get ready to leave their rooms. Restaurants were closed and food was served from our staff cafeteria in the basement of the building. Guests were restricted to only the ballroom, the lobby and the indoor public restrooms. They were not allowed to go outside. No alcohol was sold in Cancun for 36 hours prior to the arrival of the storm in an attempt to avoid drunken tourists from being injured before the storm hit. Just a few hours before the hurricane hit the city, our hotel was completely sealed by the maintenance team who closed and protected all entrances.

George, our Kids Club supervisor, had planned great entertainment in the middle of the lobby where we would normally do the guest check-in and checkout. George's main goal was to entertain the guests before the storm. It was the beginning of the evening and he and his team developed a wonderful atmosphere with music and a salsa class. This energized the guests who were smiling and forgetting the difficult night we were prepared to face in the hours to come. Guests were ecstatic, and I think George gave a great lesson to literally everyone - guests, staff, managers, and me. We couldn't control what was coming, but we could choose our response. We could decide to create the best atmosphere, relax guests, and most importantly, give them the feeling that the team was prepared, knew what to do, and could be trusted.

A month prior to the storm, we had organized a 2-day training for the entire team with an outside expert. The preparation was done with a great deal of effort and dedication so fortunately we were ready.

We served a nice dinner in the staff cafeteria to everyone and had a communication meeting with close to 200 people. The ballroom was set up with beds; there was nothing else we could have done. And, of course, George and his entertainment team created a wonderful out-of-this-world atmosphere while we were all waiting for the impact. He set the tempo and made everyone happy after 48 hours of very intense preparation.

George was a good reflection of the team spirit of the hotel. He was professional, reliable, and a hard worker. But beyond that, he provided guests with relaxation, fun and a great Cancun experience.

The high winds produced by Emily caused considerable damage in the state leaving nearly 200,000 residences without power. The most substantial losses associated with the hurricane stemmed from the tourism industry, with hotels experiencing $88 million in damages. More than 12,500 rooms, nearly one-fifth of the state's available hotel infrastructure, sustained damage. Striking the Yucatán Peninsula on July 18th as a Category 4 hurricane, widespread damage was expected from nearly 135 mph winds; however, these winds were confined to a small area around Emily's center.

Due to the relatively fast movement of Emily, rainfall was fairly light. Additionally, waves reached 13 feet resulting in some beach erosion and damage to dunes. Luckily for us, the fact that the hurricane passed slightly to the south and moved faster than anticipated (giving strong winds and less rain), was great news for us in Cancun.

Once the hurricane passed, we needed a fast recovery. We cleaned and put our efforts in area by area, pool by pool, restaurant by restaurant. We had to remobilize the staff available that had not been directly affected by the storm. The team was strong and what made it even more special was the support of our guests.

The guests that were with us during the hurricane spent the first day helping us clean the resort. It made such an impact, that we were able to return to a nearly normal operation within 48 hours. Nothing had created a better teambuilding exercise than a real event - going through a hurricane. When you have been through that type of experience, it is more than a staff–management relationship. It's a TEAM of people working together to provide the best experience possible to its guests.

So, what helped us handle Emily so well? We had hurricane policies and procedures in place that had been developed throughout the years since the hotel's opening. The head of security updated the manual constantly and had specific training for his team and each department.

At the beginning of each hurricane season, a meeting was scheduled with each department head to be sure plans were in place in case of a hurricane. In June 2005, we did an extensive 2-day workshop on how to be prepared and trained to operate in case of a hurricane - from preparation, to transformation of the hotel, from menu, to survival to aftermath recovery. Every detail was reviewed including rules and regulations of the hotel during an event when the hotel is turned into a shelter. And if we had to move inland, we learned how to change a school into a shelter. We did all the exercises, the preparation, communication, and division of roles and responsibilities. I am so grateful this training took place just a few weeks before hurricane Emily. Without a thorough preparation and the staff member commitment, it wouldn't have been possible.

Hurricane Emily taught us so much.

We learned:

Preparation: We were prepared, trained and ready to face the storm. You can't anticipate when and how a hurricane will hit; however, you and your team can be trained with a clear idea on what to do once it strikes. A very good preparation is the key to a prompt recovery.

Clear roles and responsibilities: You should make sure everyone knows his role and responsibility before, during and after the hurricane. Train both yourself and your team, and don't forget to keep everyone updated. Once you have achieved this, not only is it much easier to make decisions, but the team can better support you. All the key people were trained and knew exactly what was expected of them. They were confident in themselves and knew how to deliver. Most importantly, they had management's trust.

Transparent communication: I realized that regular, open, and clear communication with the guests, team members and owners was essential to keep everyone aligned on the situation – weather forecast updates, food menus, activity programs and basically what to expect next.

How to be one team: Those three days are still vivid in my memory, but also strangely enough, I have nice memories. It was probably one of the most interesting times in my hotel career, being in total "communion" with the team. I felt complete commitment from each team member. I was supported by everyone and knew we would be fine. I felt that the guests believed the same.

Investing in your team is the answer: Training allowed us to be proactive, adapt ourselves to the situation quickly, and eventually reopen our resort the day after the hurricane. The response from the guests was so positive, that the remaining part of the season and financial year were lucrative. We didn't have to face the consequences many resorts had to face that didn't invest as much in their staff development training and satisfaction.

Team first: From this experience I learned to always place the team first, to provide open communication, invest in solving team issues, encourage training, and develop trust between the staff and management as soon as possible.

What about you? Who is on your team? Do you have simple strategies to hire better, to get clear team communication, to get simple and transparent feedback? What would you need to do right NOW to get a winning team within the next 12 months? Do you have a plan for that? Have you hired, trained, and developed a winning team? Or at the very least, have you started to work and focus on your people? Are you ready to IMPROVE your team? It is never too late.

In the next chapters, you will find some useful and simple tools to implement ways to make your team strong and supportive of each other; things to do when faced with the unexpected. When you want to improve the quality of your product and service, it's easier with a happier team - a team that will be sure to give guests the best experience, so they stay loyal to the hotel brand. As a result, your business will grow.

A happier team will be sure to give guests the best experience, so they stay loyal to your hotel brand.

So, your first line of defense is your team. From my experience in both hospitality and business coaching, I will share with you some simple, easy strategies and techniques to improve your team's communication, leadership tools, and how to have management success that will help motivate your team.

This book is a combination of two of my passions - work experience in the hotel industry and business coaching. After my studies in Switzerland, I spent 20 years in the hotel industry in three different companies (two international brands, and one independent owner) in 10 different countries from the Middle East, Africa, Asia, the Caribbean, and North, South & Central Americas.

Over the last eight years, I have become a certified business coach, an entrepreneurial trainer and a team coach. I have combined and shared in this book what I have learned during my experience from these two passions. I have made mistakes throughout the years and learned a lot from them. I hope you will find some interesting tools you could apply in your business to improve and lead your team better.

Happiness at work reduces burnout by 125%
Happiness at work reduces sick leave by 66%
Happiness at work reduces turnover by 51%

If you are not yet convinced in investing time to read this book and to learn simple strategies for a happier team, here are more benefits that happiness at work could do for your business:

Happiness at work increases innovation by 300%
Happiness at work increases retention by 40%
Happiness at work increases sales by 37%
Happiness at work increases productivity by 21%

This book in divided into three main parts:

BUILD your team

Start with these three steps: a one-page plan including a 3–5-year vision, 12-month goals, and a 90-day plan. Review who is on your team, who to train, coach and develop or incent and, more importantly, who should be removed.

Efficiently select the best people to join your team through three interview processes.

GROW your team – you will be taught:

Three ways to grow your team through simple and clear communication.

How to coach, strategize and support your direct reports.

Four ways to make decisions and delegate.

IMPROVE your team – you will learn:

Five ways to get feedback from your team and how to use this gift.

How to get aligned with your direct reports in terms of coaching, support, and direction.

What activities you should do based on the skills and enjoyment you have in doing them.

I certainly hope by now you are convinced that this two-hour reading investment is worth your time.

Chapter Two

CARIBBEAN NIGHTMARE: WHAT YOU WANT TO AVOID

A few years after Hurricane Emily, I had a totally different experience. It was at the beginning of the 2008 financial crisis, and we knew that the following months and possibly years would be challenging. I went through a taxing experience when the team and the hotel somehow over-promised and under-delivered.

A hotel that is all-inclusive is when you pay in advance for all services, rooms, food, beverage, entertainment, and activities. It was made popular in the early 1970s by Club Med and required a high percentage of occupancy to generate profits. Our hotel had some great financial years, enjoying a high rate of repeat and loyal customers; however, it wasn't reinvesting sufficiently enough to have a high standard product, while keeping some savings for more challenging times.

After heading the all-inclusive properties on the island, the hotel needed a facelift, a maintenance investment to improve the overall experience. When the financial crisis started, we didn't have the necessary Small Operating Equipment (SOE) to have a smooth operation. When 90% of the rooms were occupied, we didn't have a full-time team to operate the hotel smoothly. Up to 70% occupancy, the hotel was doing very well, with a smooth operation and necessary team members to provide a quality experience and guest satisfaction. However, for an all-inclusive, having a 70% occupancy was not enough to break even, let alone see a profit.

With the occupancy rates not being enough, the sales team manage / supervise by the hotel owner used to make some great last-minute deals, and suddenly with only a two-week notice, the hotel was moving from a well-planned 70 to 75% occupancy (with litle profit) for the season, to 90 to 100% without having the time or the resources to buy equipment needed at the right price and on time.

It didn't give us the time to recruit, train, and have the necessary team members in place. The dangerous strategy to increase revenue by increasing occupancy with low rates placed the operations team in a huge challenge. We were not ready. We were working under a tremendous amount of stress, facing constant customer complaints, and exhausting and frustrating department heads who was not able to support the team members with sufficient tools and manpower to make sure our guests were satisfied. We were over-promising on the sales and under-delivering on the actual experience.

How do you think the team felt at the end of the season? Exhausted, stressed, demoralized, frustrated, and feeling hopeless. Of course, the staff turnaround was high. Team members were looking for better opportunities. On top of all that, our financials had declined. We were barely breaking even, without mentioning the guest's dissatisfaction. The reputation of the resort was negatively affected.

The consequences to the employees:

- Employees didn't have the necessary tools to operate properly above 80% occupancy.
- The sales team under the direction of the hotel owner made last minute deals to maximize revenue without taking into consideration what the team was able to give to the customers.

The not-so-good idea:

- Do a last-minute marketing campaign in our two main sales markets (USA & UK) with big discounts on prices.

For example, at the beginning of June, the forecasted average was 75% for July and August. Suddenly within a week, there were massive last-minute bookings that reached nearly full occupancy.

We were over-promising on the sales and under-delivering on the actual experience.

The results:

- Insufficient tools: Being located on an island, last minute resources are not so easy to get.
- We suddenly didn't have enough equipment and not enough team members.
- We had to spend a lot of time and energy in "firefighting" operational issues.

The team was negatively affected:

It resulted in an exhausted staff, low morale, and an increase in sick days. Human Resources had to quickly find underqualified staff that we didn't have the time to properly train. The team was physically and emotionally exhausted by the end of the season.

Poor customer service:

The lack of planning and anticipation resulted in a poor customer experience that led to an absurd increase of cost to provide a better guest experience. We had to make a lot of room changes as 100% of the rooms were not up to the standard. We were promising free trips, room upgrades, discounts, and a free night for future stays.

No financial reward:

We had some poor social media comments over a peak period, damaging the hotel brand and affecting future potential booking and revenue.

This is exactly the opposite of what you should do to have a happy team, to have delighted customers and to generate more profits. To avoid this nightmare scenario, you will find in this book some simple key strategies you will be able to implement in your operation to *BUILD*, *GROW* and *IMPROVE* your team.

I have found that most people who have worked with teams and on teams have had some great experiences, but some not so great. As a coach, I sometimes had clients who told me that it was too much work to build, grow and improve a team, and that they couldn't afford the time and the cost of doing so. I agree it is not something you could do in few days and without a great deal of effort but investing the time and focusing on your team is ALWAYS worth it.

Let's consider now the opposite. Could you afford to have an ineffective team in the long run? Let's be realistic. Poor teamwork affects the overall operation of your business. Think about your career as a manager.

Have you had to face the following?

- A high percent of absenteeism.
- Not being able to find the right staff for your operation.
- A struggle to keep the best team members.
- Finding yourself in constant recruiting mode.
- How to stop the vicious cycle of your team draining you with its negativity?
- Having staff issues affecting guest satisfaction?
- Having demotivated team members?

Does this sound all too familiar?

On the contrary:

- When is the last time you have been surrounded by a happy team? How did you feel?
- Have you ever been supported by a team that developed a contagious positive energy?
- Have you had a team that worked hard on sales for your hotel, welcomed customers, and supported the suppliers and local community?
- How would it be if you could reduce the staff turnaround, give you the time to train, to coach and promote your team members, and allow you to have a good succession plan?
- How would you like to be able to delegate more and have more time for yourself or focus on other priorities such as expenditures or new business development?

Part 1: BUILD Your Team

The stories from the first two chapters have shown you the impact of the team on the overall operation of a business. The first step is to now work on your team. Why? They are the ones who serve and deliver your product to your guests, the ones dealing directly with the end user. A non-professional, unfriendly or inconsistent service will have a negative, direct impact on the guest experience and therefore on your operation, which will eventually affect your revenue and bottom line. Focusing on making sure you BUILD, GROW and IMPROVE your team members, making sure they are happy in their work environment, and happy to serve your guests every day, is the priority. So where do we start?

Chapter Three

STRATEGY #1 CREATE A ROADMAP

STRATEGY #1

VISION-GOALS-PROJECTS-ACTIONS

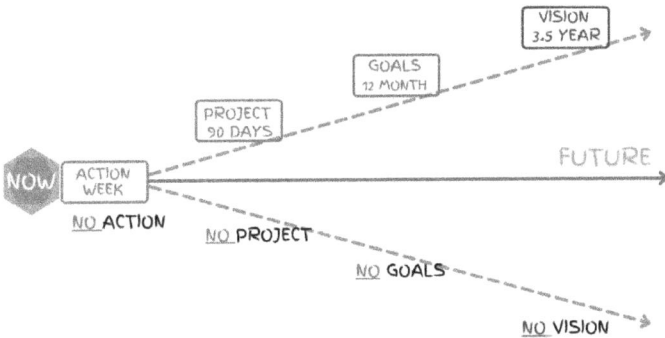

3-Year Vision, 12-Month Goals, 90-Day Plans

When you are a team leader, you need to get clarity and develop a roadmap. Until you have a vision and set goals, it is difficult to have a clear path. You need a roadmap to help your team develop a great plan.

Think of using Google Maps. You input the destination address. Google gives you the directions until you arrive at it. We do the same with the 1-page roadmap. We decide first where we want our team to be in 3-5 years and we follow the roadmap.

When we want to create and develop a team, we need to make sure the team understands, knows and agrees to the next month's goals. What are the common team objectives? What are we here to achieve?

I have worked with Patrice, a business owner in France who is in partnership with his two brothers. Philippe, the oldest, is one of the top cheese masters (affineur) in France; Eric, the youngest, takes care of the administration and finance; and Patrice manages one of the most famous traditional local restaurants in the region.

They decided to make a change.

When the three brothers decided to start exporting the cheese, they decided that Patrice, who was in charge of the restaurant, would take the responsibility of the exportation. In addition to a full-time job as restaurant owner, he started to travel extensively to the Middle and Far East. Patrice was involved actively in two different and successful businesses - one in his hometown, another one that required traveling far away for a period of three to five weeks, four to five times a year. Despite the jetlag of traveling, he was catching up with the urgent matters in France. He was coming home after 30 days, tired from all his business travel.

A few issues arose. Being away, Patrice had to delegate more and trust his triumvirate (three heads of department team) - the chef in charge of the kitchen, the restaurant manager leading the service team, and the administrative person who was taking care of the office. Patrice would work solely and directly with those three people, making him the communication liaison and solving problems day-to-day.

This week-long absence had inevitably had an influence on the day-to-day business. Each person on the team was taking responsibility of his own department, but the communication between administration and operations was not smooth, mostly due to a lack of clear goals and ineffective communication. This led to some misunderstanding tension and frustration.

In addition, the team was used to taking initiatives during the owner's absence and once the owner was back for a period of few weeks, the three managers didn't know what their roles were. Should they not be taking the initiative when the owner was there or did the owner expect them to take the lead on every matter?

Patrice contacted me and we agreed I would come and spend two days working with his team on defining a 3-year vision, 12-month goals, and a 90-day week-by-week action plan.

At the end of the two days each of them had a clear understanding of his/her own roles and responsibilities, a better understanding of the other managers' needs, a very clear 90-day, (12-week-by-week action plan), and 7-8 key goals for the business for the next 12 months.

This simple exercise had a huge impact on the three managers. Patrice was able to go on long business trips knowing that the team had better communication, clear vision on the midterm objective, and clarity and understanding of the action plan and responsibility. Most of the issues were solved by the manager who started to communicate more efficiently and regularly.

The managers decided to spend some time changing departments for a day to better understand the other managers' roles and responsibilities. A better understanding of the others' needs helps to increase teamwork. Eventually, the entire staff was less stressed as they felt and saw the increase in cooperation and support between the managers.

They decided to have a weekly meeting to review achievements from the previous week. They checked to be sure there was nothing pending and prepared the next week's goals. At the end of the 90 days, all plans were achieved, including revenue and profitability without having the involvement of the owner who was able to focus on the cheese exportation. With this simple exercise, the team was able to stay focused for the following 12 months and they reached 100% of the eight 12-month goals they had decided on during the two-day workshop.

Below shows how you can do this exercise with your team:

Your 1 Page Plan Name: Date.	
3 years 5 years 10 years [circle one] – Vision	12 months – Goals
90 Days – Projects	This week – Actions [Weekly Renewable Post-it note]

The 1-Page Roadmap - Where Are You Going?

- Develop your hotel's 3–5-year vision.
- Have clear 12-month goals.
- Have a simple 90-day plan with week-to-week goals.
- Make a vision board.

A better under-standing of others' needs helps to increase teamwork.

One of the first steps in developing a team is to be clear on where you want to go, develop a vision for your business, and decide with the team what you want to achieve. What is the three-to-five-year vision for your team, hotel or business? The steps below will help you get clarity for your future, help you with your 12-month goals, help get 90-day plans in place, and finally show your team how to make a 12-month vision board.

Step 1: 3-5 Year Vision

Work with your team and decide on a common 3–5-year vision for your hotel. Select five to eight main topics such as revenue target, new products and services or an upgrade to those that currently exist (such as a new restaurant, a spa, limousine service, butler service, entertainment or communication), a new accreditation? a specific Human Resource objective, a new geographic target market? (example, Chinese, Japanese guests), golf guests. Whatever you decide as a target to reach in 3-5 years will have a direct impact on the decisions you will make with the team.

Let's suppose you notice you have a demand for spa treatments and you either bring an outside therapist in or you direct your guests to a nearby spa. You realize you may be sending guests to your competition and miss some revenue opportunity If you decide to open a spa in the next 24 months, you want to develop a design, build it, and recruit staff. This will attract a new market of guests with different needs.

You might start to work on having, for example, a new Spa menu in your restaurant, welcome amenities, etc. You can see that a 3–5-year vision will give you clarity and will have an impact on what you are doing for the next 12 months. It is important that your team share the same vision. If your chef is not interested in the new market you're about to focus on, you will probably have to change either the objective or the chef. The vision will directly influence your recruitment and the atmosphere of the hotel.

Here are eight objective examples for your vision and goals:

1. Revenue and profitability
2. Products and services

3. Human Resources
4. Guest experience
5. Marketing
6. Environment
7. Local community
8. Developing a Unique Selling Proposition (USP)

Step 2: 12-Month Goals

When you have decided on your eight objectives for the next three to five years, you focus only on your next 12-month goals. You narrow your focus on a closer range, using the same topics from your vision, but narrowing your objective to the next 12 months.

For example, let's say your guest satisfaction is today at 70%. Your team agrees with you that this has a huge impact on the overall business and to reach your financial objective, you would have to improve the guest satisfaction to 90% within the next five years. In order to be at 90% in five years, what is your goal for the next 12 months? Maybe 80%? 77%?

Here's what you do. Your 5-year vision is to bring the guest satisfaction rating to 90%. Your 12-month goal is 77%, so then maybe your 90-day action plan goal is 73%. For your weekly action plan, you would decide what your action(s) should be for the current week to be able to get at least one more point. Maybe you would start with a complete review or assessment of your guest satisfaction rating breakdown by area or by department. If you already have all the data, schedule a meeting to analyze the data and do a team brainstorming session to improve your score. (You will learn the Start, Stop, and Keep Feedback session in Chapter 9).

Step 3: Project 90 days – 12 weeks

Do the same exercise as in Step 2 for your 12-month goal breakdown. You would break it down to the next 12 months in four periods of 3 months/12 weeks/90 days. The focus is now on just 90 days – only achievable projects in the next 12 weeks.

Step 4: Actions – Weekly

This is the last stage. Each department head knows very specifically what needs to be achieved by the end of next quarter. The department head meets with his team to break down each project over the next 12 weeks. For more clarity, you could color code – maybe one color per goal over the next 12 weeks, or color code by the person in charge of the weekly action – you decide what the best fit is for your team.

Step 5: Implement a Weekly Meeting

Once a week during a briefing or a weekly meeting, remind the team of the action for the week.

By doing this exercise you and your team are setting your Reticular Activating System (R.A.S) in the right direction. What is RAS and what does it do? Your brain is amazing and setting your focus on goals is a powerful way to harness its massive energy and power. There is a network of nerves in the brain that control the state of awareness and attention. This system functions as a filter or doorway to accept and reject the overwhelming stimuli that we all encounter when we are awake. A person can actively set this filter by choosing to think about certain things, or it will be set by the environment. One of the most familiar examples is when a person buys a new car. It seems that when you get that new car, suddenly many cars just like it appears everywhere you go! They were really there all the time, you just never noticed them until now. Why is that? It is because you have set your RAS to look for that make, color, and model of car. When we choose to set our RAS, we set the direction of our behavior. This is why goalsetting is an effective way to direct your life in a desired direction.

When you set goals and keep them top of mind, your mind is constantly looking for ways to bring those desired outcomes to pass. You are entering a new 12-month goalsetting, and it is the perfect time to place the thoughts in your mind of what you and your team would like to become, and then watch it come to pass. We truly do become what we think about.

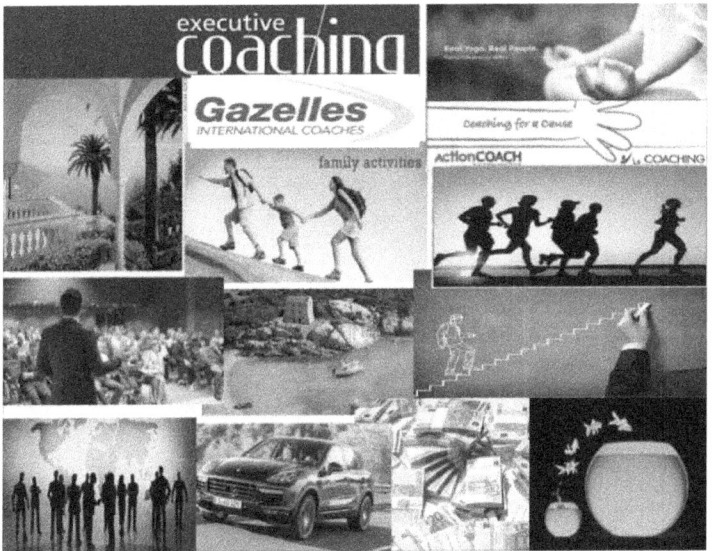

Sample of a 12-Month Vision Board

Now you and the team have some clarity on where you want to go. You have your business vision. With your team, you have defined a pathway on where you would like to be in 12 months, having set some challenging one-year goals. You can review and see who is on your team. We will see that process in our next chapter.

Your Strategy #1 Action PLAN

1. Decide a date and schedule a team strategy meeting to develop your 1-page plan starting with the vision, a one-year goal, a 90-day plan and your week-to-week actions.

2. To make it more tangible and inspiring, some teams will also do a vision board to illustrate the 1-year goal. Take your eight goals, symbolize/describe the best ideas, then make a poster with pictures that illustrates them.

3. Decide with the team on an incentive, a reward for everyone if the team reaches all the one-year objectives.

Chapter Four

STRATEGY #2 KNOW YOUR TEAM

Who Is on Your Team? The Performance and Value Matrix

Assess Your Team

Why will this process be of great benefit to your team and your organization? At the end of the exercise, you will have a clear idea of who (if any) you need to remove from your team, and you will learn if you have a negative leader. On the other hand, it will become clear who you need to invest your time in, develop who has the potential to be your leader, and who your future key team players are.

We are about to see who is on your team and how you can give a clear plan to each member to reach their goals. Have you ever questioned yourself on how to recognize your strengths and what you should do with them? More importantly, who has the potential to be the best team players for the next few months/years? What should you do to utilize their strengths and how do you keep them on your team? On the contrary, who should go because if they stay, they will only negatively affect the team spirit, lower the guest satisfaction rating, and ultimately affect your overall revenue and profitability?

Recent research completed by Bradley University studied two management models offered in literature as methodologies for increasing organization and managerial performance. The model you will see below inspired by Jack Welch, CEO of General Electric, championed the use of the Performance-Values Matrix for classifying managers. After years of experience and trial and error, he understood that the best managers not only "deliver on their commitments," but also do so in a way that is consistent with the organization's values.

Bradley University examined the comparison between the Performance-Values Matrix Model championed by Jack Welch (PVM) and the Values-Based Model (VBM) by studying 125 managers' performance at a large manufacturing organization.

A key takeaway from this research is that the VBM model may be an artifact of organization processes and not an accurate measurement of managerial performance. The results from the study provide conclusive evidence that the PVM model pushed by the General Electric CEO is both an accurate and effective tool. Leadership should view Performance and Core Values as two distinct elements of enhancing organizational performance.

What Is the "Science" Behind Performance Values Matrix?

In the Performance-Values Matrix (PVM) model there are two independent dimensions; Core Values are plotted on the X axis and Performance is plotted on the Y axis.

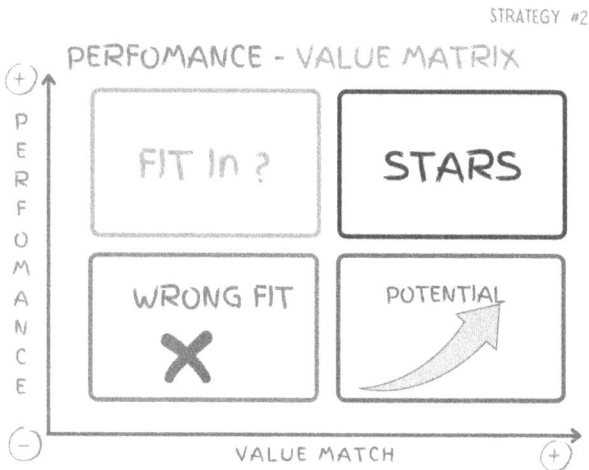

PERFOMANCE - VALUE MATRIX

FIT In ?

STARS

WRONG FIT

POTENTIAL

PERFOMANCE

VALUE MATCH

Performance is measured by the impact the employee's performance has on the company. The Core Values are measured by how an employee's behavior aligns with an organization's core values. After looking at the PVM, it may seem obvious that Performance and Core Values being separately measured is the best way to view overall employee performance. After all, we should be able to distinguish between results and how those results were achieved. Though most employees care what leadership thinks of them, they are actually quite astute at paying attention to what leadership does, not what they say.

According to the theory of behaviorism, no behavior will persist long term unless it is being perpetuated by either a positive reinforcer (providing a reward, such as a promotion or praise) or a negative reinforcer (removing a punishment, such as a probationary period or undesirable tasks).

Thus, when companies start, leaders set the company's values not by what they write on the walls, but by how they actually act. For example, do they stay late and burn the midnight oil, or do they leave early to be with their families? Those behaviors become socialized, and rank-and-file employees who take their cues from these leaders, act and react accordingly. These are what's called trickle-down behaviors.

As the company grows and senior leadership is not always readily observable, employees begin to act according to what their managers either actively reinforce through praise and promotion, or passively reinforce by allowance. Over time, employees become aware of which colleagues are being hired, fired, or promoted, and why. Your company's employees practice the behaviors that are valued, not the values you believe.

Let's see how you could use the Jack Welch System to determine who would be the stars - the one who would need to be recognized for their outstanding contribution to the company, who would need to be supported by the company, and who should be let go. He asked his HR team to build a matrix, looking at performance and value match. The matrix is divided into four quadrants, as shown below:

Q1 - Low performance and low value match.

Q2 - High performance and low value match - rotten apple, works solo, focuses on themselves and not on the team, doesn't care about team or hotel performance, is only focused on his/her results which are often negative, challenges the supervisor constantly, and has a bad overall influence on the team.

Q3 - Low performance and high value match - very supportive, committed, responsible, accountable, loyal, but not technically yet at the level you would like. They have good behavior but are not productive in quantity and quality as the top performer. Typically, new team members are usually placed in this quadrant.

Q4 - High performance and high value match - they are the stars of the company, the ideal team members, you don't want to lose them.

Behaviors - Attitude – Culture fit

Performance & Value Match	Company Name:		Date:

High performance & Low Value — Align?	High Performance & High Value — Star
Employee is achieving goals but his attitude & behavior is not matching the company culture and is affecting negatively the team	Employees achieve performance + great team player
It is usually more difficult to coach on attitude & behavior than on performance	Actions:
	career advancement & continuous improvement.
Action :	Potentially a mentor for other team members
1 - Try Coaching should focus on attitude & Changing behavior	Important help star employees achieve their personal vision
2 - Fire + "Shoot in Public "	Potential Reward incentive plan, monetary, time, recognition, Promotion if possible and / or appropriate (make sure they are able, prepare and they want)
3 - Make sure you have follow all process before firing	
4 - Make the statement to the team you don't allow this behavior & attitude in your business	•Do you have an organization chart? succession plan...
	•Coaching for the first month after a promotion

Low Performance & Low Value — Right fit ?	Low performance & High Value. — Potential
Employee does not demonstrate behaviors & attitude desired	Employee demonstrate good attitude but not yet achieve desire performance
Does not achieve performance expected	Actions:
Often keep on team too long	Coaching should focus on skills & knowledge.
Actions:	Employee will probably become a stars if have the capacity to learn & perform
1. **Fire + No Hire**	Maybe explore if another position suit better the employee
2. Does the business has core values – expected attitude ?	**Train , coach & develop**
3. How is your Hiring process ?	•Annual Appraisal ?
4. Group interview	•Training & development needs ? plan?
5. How could you check candidates behavior & attitudes?	

Identify people reporting directly to you - usually a maximum of 12. Take a few minutes and do the exercise, placing each of them on the matrix. Now let's look at the recommendation from Jack Welch's team.

Q1 - Right Fit? Fire and No Hire

Of course, before letting a team member go, you would have had all levels of communication, performance evaluations, 1-on-1 discussions to talk about issues and lack of motivation. Once you have done all your homework and it is definitively not a good fit for you, make the decision to remove this person from the team.

From this quadrant we need to spend some time on the recruitment system. Three simple ways to improve your recruitment system: deselect with a phone interview, select best candidates in the group interview and use my top 25 questions in the next chapter to identify the candidate that deserves to work for you.

Q2 - Not Aligned? Fire and Tell the Team Why

This quadrant is very challenging for business owners and team leaders. The employee delivers and achieves goals; however, his attitude negatively affects the team. Try to coach and change the behaviors. If that doesn't work, move quickly to the actions discussed in Quadrant 1. You will have to let this team member go.

In addition, discuss with your team why this person can no longer work with them - not because of quality of the work, but for lack of having the same values as the business and the team and negative leadership. Reinforce your value.

There's one more step to check before you make this decision. Have a meeting to see if this team member is committed to aligning himself/herself to your values.

Q3 - Potential - Develop, Train and Coach

Q3 requires most of your focus, time, and energy. This is the person who you will be helping you grow and will help you build your team and grow your hotel. They need to have a simple but clear plan prepared by you where they can clearly see the path for growth, learning, technical knowledge, leadership, management, and languages. They are the future of your excellence.

Q4 - Stars: How to Keep Them?

Promote your stars if possible or incent them, continue to develop them, and give them more responsibilities.

Invest in career advancement and continuous improvement. Help your star employees achieve their personal vision. Promotion is not the only way to keep your top employees. Sometimes you have no position available, or maybe he/she isn't interested in moving up. In that case, find out their needs and wants.

Financial reward should not be the only incentive. Some team members may be happy with recognition, extra days of vacation, cross-training within or outside your hotel, reduced hours, or on the contrary, working overtime to increase their income.

This exercise will identify who is on your team, who you want and need to invest your time in, where you need to invest your time, and the plan on how to develop your team. This is a good way to BUILD your team.

Your Strategy #2 Action:

In the next two weeks, do this exercise with your team:

- Define who is in which quadrant.
- Make a simple development plan for each quadrant and each team member.
- Put this plan into action to BUILD your team.

Chapter Five

STRATEGY #3 TEAM SELECTION AND DE-SELECTION

25 Questions to Select Your Next Team Member

Hotels might sell rooms, but relationships are the real currency.

The people component of the framework encompasses all the people who play a part in your hotel concept. That means your guests, your partners and, to a certain extent, your investors. More important, however, are your team members. Together they bring your concept to life. In most hotels, people are at the core of all interactions.

All too often, managing people is seen as a purely operational issue, primarily centered around skill training to increase quality and consistency of service. But intangible elements, like beliefs and shared values, can also significantly impact the customer experience.

People are at the core of all hotel interactions. The key point you should consider when hiring is to collaborate with them. They must feel connected to your story, to your vision, and to your goals. This is the reason why you want to do what we have covered in the previous chapter - set your yearly goals with your team. Before starting your recruitment process, use your RAS (see Chapter 3) and search for the team members that have the attitude that best fits your team.

What attitude would you like your team members to demonstrate with consistency? These attitudes should be a gauge for new or current team members ... the more the better!

I have summarized 18 points that demonstrate a great team member attitude. You can, of course, add a few more that will match your team expectation.

1. When coming through the recruitment stage, they offer to come and work pro bono for a time to earn the job.
2. They work to improve themselves.
3. They want to attend training external to the business and may offer to pay for part of it.
4. They have happy dispositions and positive outlooks.
5. They talk positively about ideas, concepts and people.
6. They always endeavor to speak the truth.
7. They agree to new ideas and strategies in a positive way, not find reasons why it won't work.
8. They are happy to set goals and strive for them.
9. They greet customers and other team members in a friendly manner.
10. They don't spread gossip about other team members. They don't talk about another person without that person being present.

11. They welcome new team members in a friendly manner.

12. They talk to their manager about issues or questions about the business or other team members in an honest, accurate way.

13. They support the leaders, not sabotage them.

14. They want to become a leader.

15. They do more than they are asked to do and contribute to the business without being asked.

16. They want to see the business grow and will be proactive about helping the team do it.

17. They see a future in the business and would like to see it grow.

18. They think of the business as their own.

You can now develop yours own for and with your team.

STRATEGY #3

TEAM MEMBER - GREAT ATTITUDE , CHECKLIST

(1)	
(2)	
(3)	
(4)	
(5)	

TEAM Together Everyone Achieves More

Invite your current team members to step up to higher standards and expect more from them than they do from themselves.

*There is no "I" in **T.E.A.M** –*

Together Everyone Achieves More

In my twenty years of working in the hospitality business in 10 different hotels, I have not found a recruitment system that suits me completely. When I started coaching business owners with the Action-COACH franchise, I was using most of their system and finding out it was saving time, and it avoided many simple mistakes we usually do in recruiting. This system has been used for 20 years by more than 1,000 coaches around the world and in more than 15,000 businesses on a daily basis. It works. Recruitment is not a perfect science. It doesn't mean you won't make mistakes in recruiting, but those simple steps will avoid many errors and will save precious time.

This may be a new way of hiring for your company. Remember this: If you don't change the system or process of hiring that you've been using thus far, you'll simply get more of what you've already got.

Following are the most important aspects of your recruitment, how to do phone interviews and conduct a group interview for some positions, along with my 25 top interview questions.

Hotels might sell rooms, but relationships are the real currency.

Four Key Principles to Remember When Recruiting:

1. Attract a large pool of applicants and you're more likely to get the right person.

2. Implement multiple levels of screening, and you'll waste less time in lengthy interviews with underqualified candidates.

3. Observe a short list of applicants performing the essentials of the position in real time and you're less likely to be surprised on their first day.

4. Assess your short list of applicants to make sure you're making an appropriate match.
   - Use the 10-minute screening phone interview.
   - Use group interviewing for non-managerial positions to select a candidate and save time.
   - Use my top 25 recruitment interview questions to make your final choice.

The 6-Step Recruitment Process

1. Think about what qualities and skills your ideal candidate would need to have.

2. Advertise for the position.

3. Figure out the best place to find your ideal candidate.

4. Save time. Screen by doing phone interviews.

5. Interview with consistency.

6. Make the offer – close the deal.

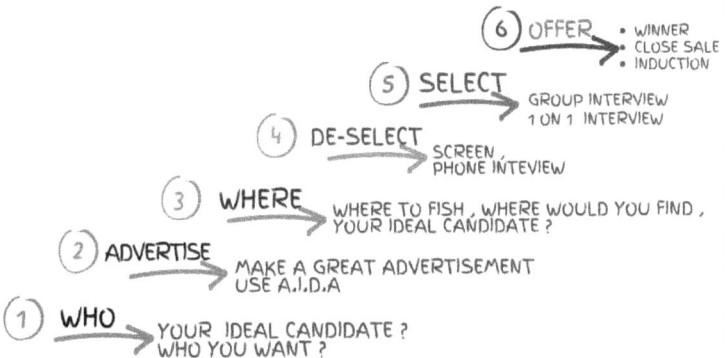

6 STEPS - RECRUITMENT

6) OFFER
- WINNER
- CLOSE SALE
- INDUCTION

5) SELECT
GROUP INTERVIEW
1 ON 1 INTERVIEW

4) DE-SELECT
SCREEN,
PHONE INTEVIEW

3) WHERE
WHERE TO FISH, WHERE WOULD YOU FIND,
YOUR IDEAL CANDIDATE ?

2) ADVERTISE
MAKE A GREAT ADVERTISEMENT
USE A.I.D.A

1) WHO
YOUR IDEAL CANDIDATE ?
WHO YOU WANT ?

Let's dive deeper into those 6 steps and then focus on steps 4 and 5.

STEP 1: Develop a clear job description for the position

1. Roles, responsibilities, tasks, duties.
2. Skills required.
3. Key Performance Indicators – what is expected from the team member.
4. Hours expected.
5. Pay range.

STEP 2: Advertise for the position - Follow the AIDA formula: Attention, Interest, Desire, Action

1. A good headline that's easy to understand.
2. The headline should be a question.
3. Focus on the benefits of the job.
4. Write in the present tense.
5. Include a call to action.
6. Always watch out for government regulations on discriminatory language.

STEP 3: Generate candidates for position

1. Look within your organization first.
2. Ask your top performing team member if they know potential candidates.
3. Use social media.
4. Offer a reward to existing team members for a successful introduction of a new member.

STEP 4: Phone screening of candidates

1. Do a 10-minute phone interview with potential candidates.
2. Rate candidates by comparing phone interview and CVs to job description.
    a. Has necessary qualifications plus other qualities
    b. Has only the necessary qualifications
    c. Missing some elements, but interesting candidate (may be of interest for a different job or another time)
    d. Not even close
3. Develop a short list of a- and b-rated candidates.

STEP 5:   Interview candidates

Arrange a group or individual onsite interview, if possible, with the short list.

1. Have candidates complete a task to demonstrate competence or key responsibilities/tasks of positions.
2. Interview candidates.
3. If possible, have one or two other people with you during the interview, maybe a staff member from the department.
4. Use the top 25 questions below.
5. Use the same set of questions for all interviewees.
6. Rate the response of interviewees on each question as 1 through 5. Record comments.
7. Rank short list according to preference.
8. Check references on top choice.

STEP 6:   Complete hiring agreement/contract

1. Negotiate salary.

2. Make a verbal offer initially by phone or face-to-face, discussing the main terms and conditions, and establishing whether or not the offer is accepted. Do this QUICKLY.

3. Offers can be made subject to candidates meeting certain conditions based on your pre-employment checks. Examples:

    a. Passing a medical examination
    b. Passing a criminal record check
    c. Providing suitable references
    d. Providing evidence of qualifications (examinations, certificates, driving license, etc.)
    e. Completing a probationary period

Don't forget to check REFERENCES

4. Carry out document checks as soon as possible and before employment commences. Most candidates won't hand their notice in to their current employer before they have a written

offer. If the candidate can't meet the conditions, you can withdraw your offer (this should be done quickly).

5. Send the successful candidate a formal offer letter including:

    a. Job title

    b. Name of person to whom the job is offered

    c. Date employment is to start

    d. Whether a probationary period is applicable

    e. The terms on which it is offered

    f. Actions required by the candidate, ex: sign and return the copy of the letter/statement of employment

6. If it is not received by their start date, candidates must receive a written statement of the main terms and conditions of employment, usually within two months of their start date.

7. Ask the candidate to send you a signed copy of the offer letter. (This establishes the terms on which the offer was made, in case of any dispute).

8. Prepare a proper induction program for the new employee.

Now that you have an idea of the six steps of recruitment, let's focus on Step 4, the phone interview.

10-Minute Screening - Phone Interview

Objective: This 10-minute phone conversation with prospective candidates is to filter out people who don't meet the minimum technical and communication skills for the job, and to identify a group of the most promising candidates to call in for the next round – either for a group or face-to-face interview.

In order to get a good comparison of candidates, they should all be asked the same questions. The score of 1 – 5 should be given against the candidate's answers on the basis of how well their answer suits them for the job. Yes, it is a subjective measure, but if it's recorded at the time the candidate gives their answer, it at least measures how you felt at that time rather than trying to remember. You may also want to make a quick note of why you gave them that score. The scores will also enable you to identify the best candidates on a more rational basis than trying to remember the impression that each one made on you or looking at vague notes to differing questions.

The objective is to quickly review the basic requirements with the candidates (qualifications, experience, availability to start, salary expected, etc.).

How: "Hello so and so, my name is Dante. You recently expressed an interest in the job advertised for XYZ. I wanted to ask you a few questions about your experience levels. It'll take about 10 minutes. Is now a good time to do that or would it be better to arrange a more convenient time for you?"

1. What interested you about the position of XYZ at our company?

2. Could you tell me a little about the main responsibilities in your current job?

3. What experience do you have? (Decide what is the most important aspect of the job.)

4. How much involvement do you currently have in dealing with guests?

5. What type of XXX work do you produce in your current job, such as XXX?

6. What level of ability would you say you have in ZZZ such as ZZZ?

7. How familiar are you with YYYY?

8. Tell me about your current salary and salary expectation?

From 1-5:

- How were their telephone manners?
- How articulate were they?
- How did their overall knowledge seem relative to the position?

Why should you do this step? This step will save you time and energy and should help you deselect candidates that do not fit in your organization or the job. You will deselect unqualified people - people who have not done the minimum research on the company or the job and just randomly sent their resume; people that have salary expectations too high for your budget; and candidates that don't have the minimum qualifications for the job advertised.

You also want to check areas not clear on the resume and do some basic verification. For example, if the job requires a driver's license, you need to verify and ask the candidate if they have a valid driver's license. If they don't, you don't waste your time in inviting someone in that doesn't match the basic job requirements. It is far better to do this additional screening in a few minutes than invite candidates only to find out you are interviewing someone that is not qualified.

Every business that I have worked with and that has added this layer in their recruitment process, has never gone back and unimplemented the phone screening interview. Once you have deselected people, you will keep your most valuable candidates for the next round - the group interview or direct face-to-face interview.

Group Interview Deselection

For certain positions, in order to save time, I have found group interviewing interesting. Most of the candidates are not used to it. This is an additional layer to select the best two to three candidates for the last round of interviews.

The Process

Now that you have selected candidates based on their resume and did another deselection with the 10-minute interviews, you should still have three to eight potential candidates. The group interview is a good strategy to save time and energy and will help you deselect some candidates to keep only the top two or three candidates to choose from. This is where you need to invest more time proceeding to the last selection and chose your best candidate.

If you still have more than three good candidates, the next step is to invite them for a face-to-face interview. If each candidate is interviewed by Human Resources, department heads, and the general manager or business owner separately, it would require a lot of coordination to plan all those interviews for each candidate. Potentially eight candidates' times three to four interviews. Do you and the others have this time available? Probably not. In addition, you might see candidates on different days which may result in a different mindset or less being focused.

For the group interview, you invite the last three to eight (maximum) candidates for the same job at the same time in the same room. In a 45-minute session, you will have some candidates that will deselect themselves, giving you the last two to three final candidates for a face-to-face interview. The group interview allows you to save time. I suggest you have two to three people from your business witnessing the interview, with Human Resources as the facilitator. In addition, I would suggest having the head of the department and a team leader from another department involved. The facilitator will conduct the interview and the two others can focus more on the answers from the candidates while observing body language, eye contact, the group dynamic, and the concentration and focus of each candidate. Having three from the business involved in the selection process also helps to get a consensus on the best candidates.

Here is the process:

- Welcome participants.
- The facilitator (Human Resources representative) introduces the people in the room, i.e., the manager, department heads, etc.
- Ask the participants if they have ever participated in a group interview.
- Explain the group interview process.
- The business owner, GM or department head quickly introduces the business (vision, values) and what the job consists of.
- The facilitator asks the first question clockwise and the second question counter clockwise to be fair. For the last two questions, you could ask for a volunteer to answer first just to observe who will take the risk, who is confidant, etc.

The facilitator will start the group interview questions as follows:

1. Now that you heard more specifics about the job, how do you think you could add value?

2. What project or tasks would you consider the most significant in your career so far? Why?

It is hard to get a good read on a candidate's degree of self-awareness and to get them to share their honest take on their weaknesses. Getting candidates to open up in a way that doesn't generate canned answers is tough. The next two questions do the trick, at least most of the time.

3. Does your current employer do performance reviews?

    a. If yes - What did your most recent performance review say were your greatest areas for growth?

    b. If no - That's too bad. It is hard to grow when you don't have good development coaching. If they had done a review, what do you guess would be two or three areas your manager would have called out as important for your growth?

4. You don't need to tell me the name, but think of one person you worked with in the last year that always gave you energy. Tell me about

them and what it is about them that worked so well for you.

5. Now, on the flip side, who was someone you respected and was good at their job but that you found draining and tried to avoid? What was it about them that didn't work for you?

6. Let's assume we both decide to move forward and you have been on the job for three months. After 90 days one or both of us decide it isn't going to work. What is the most likely reason this has happened?

7. Any other questions from the panel, manager and co-worker.

Thank the participants for their time and interest and inform them of the next step in the interview process. Tell them they have a 15-minute break, offer them a drink, and let them know that after the break, you will ask a few candidates to stay a little bit longer to ask some specific questions regarding their resume and that it will require a face-to-face private interview.

Head into a feedback meeting. The two to three people that have observed the interview and the facilitator share and justify their selection and choice. Selection of the top two or three candidates stay for a face-to-face interview.

Often after the first 20 minutes in a group interview, you will clearly see the room dynamic - which candidates have more personality, the leader, the one who thinks he has to show his sense of humor, and the way they interact with each other. You will have a more accurate selection of the person you would like to have on your team.

What have I learned from those group interviews?

1. I have found the group interview particularly interesting to use when you have many candidates to choose from, when you need to deselect in a short period of time, and when you want to observe the candidate in a "team" environment.

2. On each occasion, I have experienced a few candidates that clearly deselect themselves by their attitude and behavior.

3. On each occasion, the best candidates are also clearly identified by the two or three people that observe the interview.

4. I always recommend the observers to justify their choice in selecting their preferred candidates, why they feel these are the top candidates for our team.

5. It is important to inform candidates during the phone interview that the next step would include a group interview and possibly a one-on-one interview and that they would need to plan between one to two hours.

6. Note: this type of interview is not for managerial position.

Now you have selected the last two or three candidates. Because the candidates are already there, I would recommend continuing the interview process, doing the one-on-one interviews. Ask specific questions regarding their resume and use the questions below to interview. I have used these questions over the years either for department head positions, general managers in the hospitality industry, or while recruiting as a business coach.

Here is an overview of what you would want to know from your candidates in 25 questions:

- Questions 1 to 6: Check the amount of time and work the candidate has invested in researching your company, the job itself, and what interested them about the job.

- Questions 7 to 15: Focus on knowing the candidate more - self-reflection on their accomplishments, performance, time management, how they perceive guests, their flexibility, self-awareness, and their area of opportunities and growth.

- Questions 16 to 18: These are not linked to the work, but to learn more about their personality (If you are lacking time, these can be disregarded).

- Questions 19 & 20: What type of management style motivates them, and on the contrary, what style they do not like. This is very important for the manager who will supervise the candidate to check if their management style matches, ex: can a candidate handle a micro-manager or vice versa.

- Questions 21 to 24: The reason for leaving their previous job could be a great way to learn about the candidate, their motivation, team-related experiences, salary, motivation, etc. Their behaviour could be the same for the next job; how motivated the candidate is with the job opportunity and the salary expectation. This should have been checked already during the phone interview.

- Question 25: To conclude, you may give an opportunity for the candidate to ask a question. It is interesting to learn what the candidate asks - something not yet covered, the job itself, the team, the supervisor, the environment, the growth opportunities within the company, etc.

25 Questions to Ask Your Candidate

1. Can you tell me about yourself?

2. What did you do to prepare for this interview?

3. Who are our three biggest competitors?

4. How will you describe the job and company to your friends and family?

5. What interested you in the job? (By the way, here's what we liked about your resume).

6. How do you think your background and talents suit this job?

7. What accomplishment are you most proud of and how did you do it?

8. We all make mistakes at times, tell me about a time when you made a mistake.

    a. What did you learn from it?

    b. What would you have done differently?

    c. How did you handle it?

9. Sometimes we have to work with extremely tight deadlines. Tell me about a time when you've been involved in a situation like that and how you dealt with it.

10. Guests can sometimes appear to be unreasonable. Can you give me an example of how you have dealt with a difficult guest?

11. Have you ever been asked to compromise your integrity by a colleague or supervisor?

12. What is the biggest problem you solved in a previous job?

13. What do you do in your job that is not covered in your job description and why?

14. If I called your current manager, what are the three words he/she would use to describe you and why would he/she choose those words?

15. What do you guess would be the 2-3 areas your manager would have recommended as important for your growth?

16. If there was one thing you could do over in life, what is it and what did you learn from it?

17. What goals do you have outside of work?

18. What is your biggest success in life. What made you choose that one to share with me?

19. Think of one person you worked with in the last year that always gave you energy. Tell me about them and what it is about them that worked so well for you?

20. Now on the flip side, who was someone you respected and was good at their job, but you found them to be draining and tried to avoid at work? What was it about them that didn't work for you?

21. Why did you leave your last job?

22. If we were to offer you the job would you accept it? If they say yes, ask why.

23. Let's assume we both decide to move forward, and you have been on the job for three months. After 90 days one or both of us decides it isn't going to work. What is the most likely reason this may have happened?

24. What is your current salary and what would be your expected salary if successful in this position? This should have been asked in the application or telephone deselection process, but a reminder just in case.

25. What else would you like to know about the job?

Your Strategy #3 Action:

1. Review the 6-step process with your team.
2. Implement steps 4 and 5.
3. In your next recruitment, use:

   a. Phone interview to deselect.

   b. Group interview when possible to save time and gain consistency.

   c. Questions from my top 25 interview questions and monitor if it helps you.

Part 2: GROW Your Team

In Part 1 we talked about a few strategies to BUILD your team. In the next three chapters, we will be focusing on strategies to GROW your team by giving them more responsibilities, giving them more tools to make decisions, saving you time, and tips on coaching your managers.

Chapter Six

STRATEGY #4 COACHING, NOT TELLING

Coaching Your Direct Reports

When I arrived in Cancun, Mexico to take the job as executive assistant manager in charge of Operations, I focused on room divisions and the spa in a 5-star resort. I didn't speak a word of Spanish. I didn't have the technical knowledge background, as my previous 12 years were more focused on food and beverage.

I was coming in with a food and beverage background but was suddenly in charge of all operations, a position I was never involved in such as room divisions, bell-boy, concierge, reception, operator, laundry, housekeeping, security and spa.

My predecessor was technically far better than me, as he knew the job and spoke the language. In addition, he had hired very highly qualified department heads, so he had developed a winning team. He was a really nice guy who was appreciated by everyone.

Holy cow! I felt as though I was going to crash within the first three months. What was I going to do? How can I have had value to this team? That was my reaction after the first 24 hours in the resort.

If I didn't succeed, it would have severe consequences within the operational team, which could affect the executive team, my relationship with the GM, and my career with Le Meridien. On another note, if I didn't make it, it would have huge consequences with my wife who was about to give up a job she had fought so hard for - a dream job, a place she wanted to work since she was 7 years old. So a crash was not and could not be in the plan.

My Strategy

I couldn't speak Spanish, so I had to listen and the best way to listen is to ask questions. When you constantly ask candid questions (I needed to learn what they were doing), it gets the employee thinking about the reason for doing a certain task. Normally the supervisor would be making recommendations, so the employee is not used to getting the questions. The employee had to think about the answer twice and not just say, "I am doing this because we have always done it," so in a sense, I was coaching management style without knowing it.

I was helping them think through without giving them direction, without judging. Employees were motivated every time I had an interaction with the department head. In strong teams, you have strong personalities and what I noticed was some department heads had difficulty communicating with each other and were not very good at managing conflict.

My second strategy was helping them through conflict sometimes between them, and sometimes with their supervisor or staff members. I became a reliable advisor, someone they could trust and who could help them think through their issues, challenges, and doubts.

After six months when I did a performance review with the general manager, to my surprise he had super positive comments asking me how I had managed to get such a positive working environment. He also mentioned that I was a great listener. If he only knew. I never told him it was my only strategy at first to survive. In the next two years, the hotel was nominated best hotel in the region and second in the world for our hotel chain in guest satisfaction. Our spa also got many top awards.

I was lucky to inherit such a wonderful department heads but we got better results because of my leadership style - being a supporter, a coach, giving positive energy, being a good listener and letting the team work independently. This leadership style got wonderful results. If I had a weak team, of course, we probably would have crashed. When you have the right people with a clear direction and you give them the tools, support, training, development, coaching, encouragement and motivation, this makes them happy.

One of the strategies to GROW your team will be coaching your direct reports. In this chapter, I will show you how to coach your direct reports one hour a week for each one reporting directly to you. If you have eight direct reports, you could split it up over four days and invest two hours per day to coach and develop them.

As a business coach, I have been using this format for many years and all my clients who have been successful in coaching, growing their teams and their business, have been great fans of this straightforward format and process. In the next section, you will learn how to use the Strategy and Support Progress Sheets that are to be filled out after each meeting.

How to Use the One-on-One Strategy and Support Progress Sheets

Week 1:

1. Overview

    a. A fundamental aspect of the success of one-on-one meetings is the requirement of your department head to use a progress report (see template). The use of the progress report should be made clear at the first meeting. You also want to remind them to have open and honest communication.

    b. This form makes the progress simpler and more consistent and should be used in conjunction with the script below.

    c. This process will show you how the form should be used, how it helps you get results with your direct reports, and what specific benefits you can expect as a result of using this procedure consistently in coaching him or her.

    d. Provide your direct report with a copy of the progress report as a template.

2. Using the Form – Step-by-Step (see illustration of form on the following page)

   a. The number one thing learned from the meeting - this is REALLY important as it gives your team member the opportunity to confirm what they have learned as a direct result of the meeting. This must be completed at the end of each meeting.

   b. Goals 1, 2, 3 – all agreed-upon goals must be identified in the sheet. The goals should adhere to the SMART principle and be aligned with the hotel/department's 90-day plan. These also ensure that your team member has understood the agreed-upon goals and that you are both in alignment.

   c. Actions for you – if you have agreed to do something, it must be recorded. This may be to send them a document, provide something, etc.

   d. Their brightest achievement – Your team member will always have achieved something positive. As their supervisor, you must identify key wins. Even if they have had a tough week, you need to find the positives in every situation.

e. Their main challenge – Your team member will have challenges, and it is important for them to share them with you so you can assist them effectively.

f. Something they've learned - It is really important that your direct report continue to learn, grow, and develop their skills and knowledge as a result of your support. Remember that learning can come from books, videos, a meeting, or a discussion, but also just living life and recognizing that lessons are available to us everywhere.

g. Their greatest focus at the moment – Again, the key here as their supervisor is to ensure that they are working not only on the day-to-day aspects of the operation, but also on their department procedures and the appropriate aspects of it.

h. As their supervisor, you can help them out – Another key area of the document. This will enable you to deliver great value at the next meeting. Remember, if your team member says it, then it is true to them.

i. What have they concentrated on? This is a key focus point to make sure that your team member is working on the appropriate area of their department/the business, and focused on improving profitability by either increasing the revenue or reducing the cost.

j. They have also worked on what? Other areas they need to focus on is developing and supporting their team such as communication, training, coaching or a long-term project. This is your opportunity to keep them on track.

3. Other Considerations

a. Keeping focused – the progress report helps you deliver consistent support to your key team members. By keeping records, it is possible to go back and review historic learning, goals, objectives, etc. This helps your team member to understand how much has changed, what they have achieved, and what the potential is for working with you as their supervisor.

b. Control – using the progress report is a point of discipline that gives regularity and structure to support your team member. It also helps to make the "invisible" coaching more tangible and visible. Using it will get your team member used to reporting in a structured way. It may be that they use a similar document with their own teams at some point.

I have been using the following format for many years:

STRATEGY #4

STRATEGY SUPPORT PROGRESS

NAME :_____   DEPARTMENT : _____

ACTION OF THE WEEK GOALS	ACHIEVE:

BEST ACHIEVEMENT:	MAIN CHALLENGE:
	SOLVE:
	PENDING:

MY FOCUS #1	AS MY SUPERVISOR YOU CAN HELP ME:

I THINK I HAVE BENEFIT FROM TODAY MEETING IS :

Strategy and Support Progress Sheets
One-on-One

Week 2

Your mindset before you start:

Passionate + Positive + Assertive + Leader

1. Start

    - Review previous notes and smile before you start.
    - Build rapport.
    - What has been happening with work this week?
    - What have they done to improve their department/people this week?
    - What would they like to cover? Outline what you have to cover.
    - Praise wins. Tell them how great they are for taking positive action.
    - Share any success stories with each other. This brings out positivity.

2. Goals

    - Review goals from last week.
        a. Did you achieve them? Discuss.
        b. Why not? Discuss.
        c. When will you complete them? They must commit to new dates.

    d. Do you see the importance of achieving this?

    e. Reinforce how great they are for taking this action.

    f. Goal 1

    g. Goal 2

    h. Goal 3

3. Strategy

- Discuss priorities for the coming week.
- Brainstorm tactics.
- Break it up into manageable and well-defined steps if needed.
- Add to goals for the coming week.

4. Learning – personal growth

- What have you been reading/listening to/watching to / observe / this week?
- What are you getting out of it?
- How are you going to apply that to your work?

5. Overall goals

- Quick review and refocus.
- Focus on their main goal and deliver it.
- Make sure all goals are SMART-tested.

6. Ending

Run through what you got out of today's session.

- Goals for this week
- What did we agree you are going to do this week? Be specific - how much, who, by when.
- Complete Weekly Goals Sheet.
- Discuss workload.
- How do you feel about the workload you have this week and your ability to get it done?
- Get commitment to do whatever it takes.
- Next week
- What would you like to cover next week?
- Confirm date and time for next meeting.
- Give praise. Always finish on a high and positive note.

Your Strategy #4 Actions:

1. Start your strategy and support one-on-one weekly meetings with your direct reports.

2. Follow the format of the meeting and use the progress report sheet. Test and measure this meeting for at least 90 days with each of your direct reports.

3. After a quarter, review the process, the format, get feedback from your team, adjust and make modifications if needed and do it again for another three months...

Chapter Seven

STRATEGY #5 4 WAYS TO COMMUNICATE

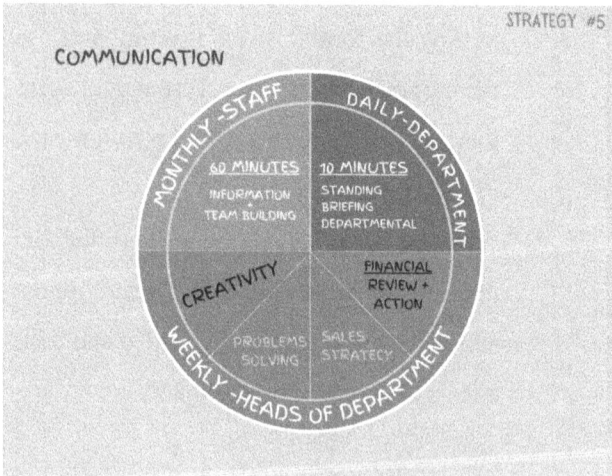

I have done and attended daily briefings in many hotels where I have worked and the one thing I never forgot was that it is a briefing, not a meeting. The object of this briefing is to share the most important information that concerns everyone - last night's occupancy, revenue, forecast of the day, any special VIP event that everyone would need to know about, or anything special happening that day at the hotel or in the city. We would also cover any urgent issues or problems that someone in the room would need to do as a priority. That was it. This is a touchpoint for five minutes, 10 max. Anything else that required more than 10 minutes is no longer a briefing but a meeting where a discussion can develop.

Usually, a briefing should be done at the start of the day with one person from each department. As food and beverage manager and director, I used to do a briefing for my own department on a daily basis. I like to do a standing briefing to give a sense that it will be brief, getting straight to the point and not engaging in a long exchange. After trying different ways, I found a daily 10-minute standing briefing and a weekly 60-minute communication or problem-solving meeting was a good balance, relaying sufficient information without wasting long hours in several meetings.

Number 2: Weekly communication and creativity – problem-solving meeting

Once a week have a department head/supervisor meeting with key members of your team depending on the number of team members in your business. Even if you have a small business and only two or three supervisors, don't rely on daily small talk. Be sure to have formal meeting minutes taken with action items noting timeframes. This meeting will allow you, your team and the business once a week or bi-monthly to get and give the most important information and decisions. I have worked in more than 10 countries and in more than 15 organizations and have seen nearly everything. All too often meetings are unproductive, long, and boring.

Try a creative meeting. Instead of doing a weekly informational meeting that might be too repetitive, you could alternate and do a creative problem-solving meeting. You take the same people in the room for 60 minutes and discuss one or two issues the team or you want to solve. Take 30 minutes per subject, or if it is a difficult one, use the full hour. Split it up into two groups, give them 15 minutes to analyze the root cause, and come back with three to five suggestions to solve the issue. Then both groups have to present their results. Make a plan of action with solutions proposed in the following two weeks. Then the team is discussing and solving the issue, not you.

Below are 13 tips for productive meetings if you have them regularly:

1. Rotate the chairperson on a weekly basis. This provides a sense of responsibility, accountability, and development. Everyone will feel more concerned and more empowered. It is also a nice way to develop a junior manager to get used to having productive, dynamic meetings. Also, it becomes the team meeting rather than the boss's meeting.

2. The chairperson in the room speaks last. Why? I have observed once the leader of the meeting has finished what he has to say, he is less focused and more impatient. It changes the dynamic of the meeting. It is perceived as the

chairperson's or leader's meeting - totally the opposite of what you want to achieve. The meeting is for your team to express, talk, tell you the issues, the problems to be solved, and what they need from you, from the others, the organization, etc. If the leader speaks last, he can use information from the meeting, combine and discuss the most important points, etc.

3. Have a timekeeper, preferably not the chairperson of the meeting. The chairperson needs to focus on the discussion and the dynamic of the meeting.

4. Start with the most important issues.

5. Have a purpose for the meeting. Arrive prepared. Begin with the end in mind. Know what you want to achieve.

6. Don't allow for cellphone interruption. A recommendation would be to have no cell phones in the room (wishful thinking maybe); however, I guarantee you a completely different dynamic and energy without cellphone usage.

7. Alternate between an informational meeting and a creativity/problem-solving meeting. Select two or three issues you want to discuss for 20 minutes and solve them. Break the team into sub-groups to brainstorm and come up with suggestions (10 minutes).

8. For one-on-one meetings or most small meetings, try to keep it to 25- or 50-minute slots to get time to review emails, take bathroom breaks, make phone calls, etc.

9. Do shorter, stand-up meetings. It will give a sense of urgency, and the speaker will get straight to the point. It's more dynamic and creates more energy.

10. Each action item needs an owner, a person responsible and accountable for the task.

11. Have a meeting between the general manager and the second-in-command once a week for one hour. You can't afford to have a dysfunctional leading team in your organization with your number two. You must have clear communication and a decision-making process to be constantly aligned in the direction, speed, and priorities.

12. Use this same format/framework across the entire organization.

13. Test and measure this for three months. Review, make change, and improve if necessary.

Number 3: Monthly staff communications and motivational meetings

In some countries in larger operations, I have also experienced the monthly communication meeting. In Cancun, on one of the last days of the month depending on our banquet room occupancy, we used to have a 45-minute gathering with the entire staff at change-of-shift time, usually 3:00-4:00 p.m., rotating which shift works the extra hour.

The objective was to:

- Have direct communication from the general manager and the executive committee to the staff. The staff heard key information directly from management and none from a second source or indirectly.

- Inform and motivate the entire team. They usually tended to have a lot of energy in the room with sound, lighting, and some simple, low-cost, but tasty food from the kitchen. This was the responsibility of Human Resources and the training department with support from our animation team. They organized the entire event.

- Have HR prepare a slideshow with the main events of the current month, VIP, internal events, main training done in the hotel, and promotions.

- Have the GM do a short 5-minute speech with what is happening, what is planned for the following month, and any other topic that needed to be shared with the entire staff.

- Have the financial controller give brief financial results of the hotel month-to-date and year-to-date, and give information pertaining to finance that mattered to everyone.

- Have the director of Sales and Marketing give positive feedback from the guests, talk about what major groups were scheduled or events were happening in the coming months, and what the next month's sales promotions were.

- Have the director of Food and Beverage give feedback on the current and following month's F&B promotions.

- Have the director of Maintenance talk about the next month's projects, renovations, etc.

- Have any other executive committee member that has something to share come on stage for two to three minutes – short talks to keep the meeting dynamic.

- Have Human Resources come last to celebrate the team members who had a birthday during the month with a large cake.

I have found this to be a very good forum to meet most of the staff in a relaxed, high energy, positive, and fun environment. Staff was informed directly and knew what was happening in the hotel.

More than 15 years later, I still remember the positive feeling I had during those meetings and some fun times shared with the entire team. Of course, this is not possible in every hotel. They seem to be easier in resorts and larger hotels. In your operation, what can you do to have a monthly or at least quarterly (for smaller hotels) event to inform, motivate, celebrate and say "thank you" to your team members?

Number 4: Virtual Meeting

For many businesses, teamwork and communication has changed radically over the last months since COVID-19 and confinement took place. In case you have to do virtual meetings, find 11 productive tips below:

1. Research and select the best technology and online tools such as Zoom, Teams, or Google Meet.

2. Establish clear rules of engagement.

3. Establish a virtual "water cooler" where casual conversation can happen and encourage collaboration (breakout rooms, etc.)

4. Create daily check-ins online so your group becomes comfortable with the format.

5. Have a clear agenda. Send it ahead of time so participants can prepare and meet with a purpose.

6. Highlight and be clear about the key points and takeaways you want each participant to have at the end of the meeting.

7. Allow adequate time for discussion and participation.

8. Share material in advance such as forecast, revenue, etc.

9. Provide an online etiquette refresher for all participants.

10. Ensure your environment, slides, audio and lighting are free from distraction so participants can focus.

11. Be a good facilitator to ensure meeting goals are achieved.

Your Strategy #5 Action:

1. Start with a daily standing briefing.
2. Alternate a team communication or creative problem-solving meeting on a weekly basis.
3. If possible, develop a monthly or quarterly staff event.
4. Give virtual meeting tips if applicable.

Chapter Eight

STRATEGY #6 BETTER DECISION MAKING

All Problems Should Be Solved by The Leader In Charge

I recommend when you have time, read the remarkable book from David Marquet, *Turn the Ship Around!* Marquet, an experienced naval officer, was used to giving orders. As a newly appointed captain of the USS Santa Fe, a nuclear-powered submarine, he was responsible for more than a hundred sailors deep in the sea. In this high-stress environment where there is no margin for error, it was crucial for his men to do their job and do it well. But the ship was dogged by poor morale, poor performance, and the worst retention in the   fleet.

Marquet acted like any other captain until one day, he unknowingly gave an impossible order, and his crew tried to follow it anyway. When he asked why the order wasn't challenged, the answer was, "Because you told us to." Marquet realized he was leading in a culture of followers, and they were all in danger unless they fundamentally changed the way they did things.

That's when Marquet took matters into his own hands and pushed for leadership at every level. *Turn the Ship Around!* is a true story of how the Santa Fe skyrocketed from worst to best in the fleet by challenging the U.S. Navy's traditional leader/follower approach. Struggling against his own instincts to take control, he achieved the vastly more powerful model of giving control.

Before long, each member of Marquet's crew became a leader and assumed responsibility for everything he did, from clerical tasks to crucial combat decisions. The crew became fully engaged, contributing their full intellectual capacity every day, and the Santa Fe started

winning awards and promoting a highly disproportion-
ate number of officers to submarine command.

No matter your business or position, you can apply
Marquet's radical guidelines to turn your own ship
around. The payoff: A workplace where everyone
around you is taking responsibility for their actions,
where people are healthier and happier, and where everyone is a leader.

I write about this because I have experienced this management style in the hospitality industry.

My first day working as a department head at a hotel in
Barbados was a Wednesday in June 2009. How do I
remember it was a Wednesday? Because every
Wednesday our resort did a beach BBQ for approximately 500 guests. It was the middle of the afternoon
and I was meeting with a department head. She was
explaining her current challenges when Jackson came
in my office. He wanted to know if he should set up the
beach BBQ on the beach or keep it inside in our main
dining restaurant.

Jackson was from Barbados and worked at the hotel for a least 10 years. He was the chief steward for the past few years, head of the department in charge of cleaning. He would also set up all our food and beverage activities and was leading a team of close to 20 team members.

On a weekly basis, his department was setting up the Wednesday guest BBQ on our main beach. This exercise requires quite a lot of coordination. The beach boys needed to clear the larger side of our beach. Lounge chairs and umbrellas were removed by 4 p.m., the beach was cleaned, and the stewarding department had a large crew set up the tables, chairs, and BBQ. It is simple work but required some logistics and coordination. However, the teams were well-trained and were used to doing it regularly for many years. It became quite a routine job to do.

I stumbled when Jackson asked me a question. I suddenly had a déjà vu as it reminded me of an experience I went through more than 15 years earlier.

On my first day as the director of Food & Beverage of a large hotel in Gabon, I received a call from the head chef. He called me after 11 p.m. to get approval on the menu du jour for the following day. I was very sleepy after the long day I had just had. The only answer I could say was, "24 hours ago I was not here and we didn't know each other, so let's pretend it is the same until tomorrow morning and you figure out the best menu. I believe as head chef you are the best person to make the decision."

15 years later here we go again. This time being in front of the department head and meeting him for the first time, I knew I had to take more time. My first question was to understand why the chief steward had to ask the general manager where the beach BBQ was supposed to be set up.

I was puzzled by his reply. "I do this every week. Each Wednesday I come and ask the GM where we should set up the BBQ. The GM decides. Yes, you are the boss, you know better. You are the person in charge of the resort, so we ask you to make the decision."

I asked him, "Who is setting up the BBQ?"

"My team," replied Jackson.

"In case of rain, who will have to do all the changes?"

"My team," said Jackson.

"Jackson are you from Barbados?"

"Yes sir."

"Did you check the weather forecast?"

"Yes, and there is a chance of rain later today."

"What is the consequence of rain?"

"It is a big mess. We have to reset and transfer 350 to 500 people from the beach to the restaurant."

"How long have you been working in this hotel ?"

"More than 10 years sir?"

"It is my first day at the hotel. Do you believe I know the weather forecast better than you and that I can evaluate the consequence of a bad decision? So, taking into consideration that I am the least qualified, could you check with the other supervisors and department heads such as the executive chef, the restaurant manager and the guest relation manager to help make the decision?"

"Yes, I can do that."

"Jackson, I trust that three or four of you are going to make the best decision. So, from now on, you will never come to ask me where to set up the BBQ, however you will discuss it with the right person and just let me know what your decision is. The only thing I might ask you to do is to justify why you have made the decision not to set up on the beach. Are we ok with that?" And it was the last time Jackson asked me where to set up the beach BBQ.

Those examples show that you as a leader of your team can't and shouldn't make all the decisions. I would say on the contrary. **All problems should be solved by the leader in charge as a way to GROW your team member.**

To be able to accomplish this, there are a few strategies in this chapter that can help you. The first would be to delegate as much as possible. Below are the five reasons and four steps of delegation:

DECISION MAKING PROCESS

- TEAM DEPEND ON YOU
- YOU ARE THE BOTTLE NECK
- NO TIME
- TAKE MOST OF DECISION

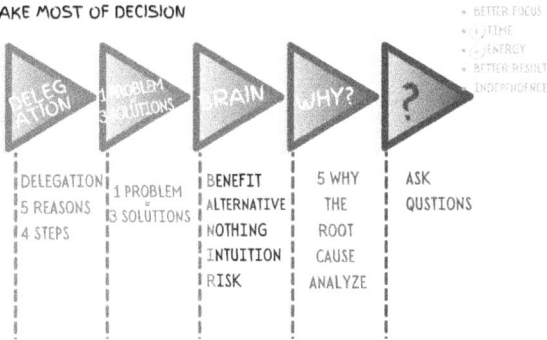

- BETTER FOCUS
- TIME
- ENERGY
- BETTER RESULT
- INDEPENDENCE

DELEGATION 5 REASONS 4 STEPS	1 PROBLEM = 3 SOLUTIONS	BENEFIT ALTERNATIVE NOTHING INTUITION RISK	5 WHY THE ROOT CAUSE ANALYZE	ASK QUSTIONS

Five Reasons Why You Want to Delegate:

1. To allow for the growth and development of your staff.
2. To teach your staff to accept more responsibility and become more valuable.
3. To improve productivity and efficiency – both of yourself and of your key people.
4. To be able to grow your team, department and business more effectively.
5. To give yourself more personal time.

The 4 Steps of Delegation:

1. Before you delegate, ask yourself, "What is the worst that could happen, and can I live with that?" If you feel that you could live with the worst that could happen, then delegate.

2. What is the cost of not delegating?
   - Compare the cost to you - your time per hour against the cost per hour of a team member (or outside source). Decide if the job should be delegated or not.

3. The process of delegation to a staff member:
   - Have a clearly defined **set of policies in place** that the staff member can refer to

for guidance and be prepared to stand behind the staff member's decisions based on those policies.

- Give them the **skills and training** needed to do the task.
- Give them the **responsibility** to take the action required.
- Give them the **authority** to be able take the action required.
- Give them a **timeframe** to complete the task.
- Give them a **clear picture** of what outcome you want.
- Give them **feedback** so they know they are producing what you want.

4. Keeping control after you have delegated. (Two different levels of delegation)
   - Level 1 - Team member is asked to look at all the options, decide, then report back

to you for your final okay before any action is taken.

- Level 2 - Team member is asked to do as above, take action, **then** report back the results of the action for your review.

Now that we know why and how to delegate, you can teach your team other ways to solve problems.

Three Potential Solutions for One Problem

Several years ago, I learned a valuable lesson about problems. I had a general manager who gave me a very important tip that would change my way of seeing a problem. My team developed a habit that began to weigh me down. Every problem that they encountered ended up in my office. It didn't matter what the problem was, they brought it to me. I wanted nothing more than to help them succeed, but I was in a catch-22. I learned that the higher you go in leadership, the harder the problems you need to solve. In order for me to serve my team best, I couldn't be constantly bogged down and interrupted during the course of the day.

So, my general manager suggested a valuable new policy: All problems should be solved by the leader in charge. If they couldn't figure it out, they could come to me but had to have three possible solutions (one of which included their input). I can't even begin to tell you how well his suggestion worked. The number of problems that hit my office was cut in half. And when my team did bring me problems, they also brought me solutions. What I learned from this is that oftentimes, our problems aren't our problems, it's our approach to problems that trip us up. How are YOU approaching problems? Are you leading through the challenge with solutions in mind?

Use BRAIN

Another simple way to help you and your team implement the, "all problems should be solved by the leader in charge" policy that I discovered while coaching, is what we would call BRAIN. This acronym stands for **B**enefit – **R**isk – **A**lternative – **I**ntuition - **N**othing.

I often use this in my toolbox while coaching and training business owners, leaders and teams. Teach your team that they can make a decision. They could review the decision using BRAIN.

Here is how it works:

B - Benefit. What would be the benefit of making this decision – benefit for the business, the department, the guest, the team.

R - Risk. What is the potential risk? What can happen? Can you live with those risks? Are they acceptable?

A - Alternative. What would be your alternative if you DON'T make this decision? Are there any other options?

I - Intuition. Deep inside what is your intuition? Is something not right? You can't explain it, but something doesn't feel right? Or is it the opposite? You feel this is the right thing to do.

N - Nothing. What would happen if I do nothing, if I don't take any action? Maybe you are not ready, you don't have all or enough information, the time might not be correct, or the team is not yet ready for this type of action.

I have shared this simple tool to many business owners and teams, and it is one of the tools they like to use because it quickly clarifies to team members when they have to make a decision while giving them some direction.

The 5 Whys - What Is the Root Cause of the Problem?

Another tool that helps problem solve and gives more clarity on how to solve an issue is using the 5 Whys. I would have loved to use and teach this to my managers and supervisors earlier in my career, but unfortunately, I discovered it too late to benefit the hotel industry. Too many times I went too fast and tried to fix the problem as I thought I understood it and too many times I just solved it temporarily or "on the surface" because I was not aware of the real problem, the root cause. I didn't search the real issue more and just assumed I understood the issue after the first answer was received.

The 5 Whys is quite simple but not used enough. Asking a question is a good method, however I was not exploring enough and asking WHY this is happening again and again and again. I should have reached a point long before where I should have known the true problem. Once the true problem is identified, more than 50% of the work is done and you can start to think of the two or three solutions you can use to address it. See the chart below and the examples used to illustrate the 5 Whys.

5 Whys for Root Cause Analysis (RCA)

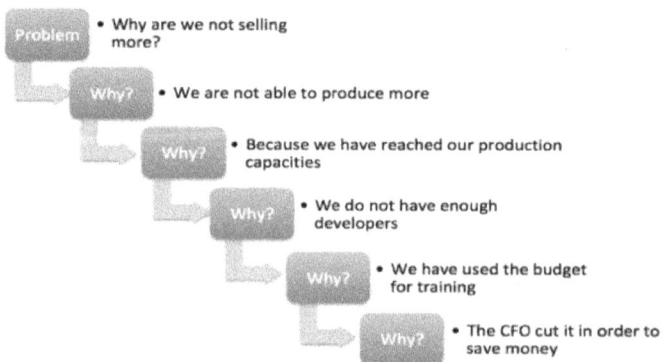

Problem
• Why are we not selling more?

Why?
• We are not able to produce more

Why?
• Because we have reached our production capacities

Why?
• We do not have enough developers

Why?
• We have used the budget for training

Why?
• The CFO cut it in order to save money

Last but not least, when communicating with your team the most appropriate way to communicate is by asking questions. Sometimes when you make a statement, someone can either agree or disagree. Instead of a statement, ASK a QUESTION.

Your Strategy #6 Action:

1. Start to delegate more.

2. Teach and apply three solutions for one problem.

3. Use and teach BRAIN to your team to guide them in making a decision.

4. Use the 5 Whys.

5. Practice "instead of making a judgment ASK a QUESTION."

6. Read *Turn the Ship Around!* by David Marquet.

7. Train your team on the three problem-solving strategies.

Part 3: IMPROVE Your Team

In this last part of the book, I will share three strategies I have used to IMPROVE teams, such as the best ways to get feedback, the seven questions of leadership and last but not least, a matrix that will help you decide how you and your key team members should spend your time.

Chapter Nine

STRATEGY #7
FEEDBACK IS A GIFT

Receiving Feedback is a Gift

Would you be interested in getting over 100 great ideas from your team to improve your business?

Are you satisfied today with the feedback and ideas you receive from your team members? Could you get more?

Do your team members give great ideas on improving their work, increasing guest satisfaction, improving internal communication, and getting better profitability? Could you imagine the positive impact that this could have on you? Your team? Your guests?

In this chapter I will show you some simple yet powerful ideas to implement in your hotel to get powerful, direct ideas from your staff that can make some positive changes for them, for your guests, and for you.

Six Ways to Communicate and Get the Best Feedback from Your Staff

1. Management to staff feedback
2. On-the-spot direct feedback
3. Monthly feedback staff dinner
4. Management swapping jobs for a day
5. Night shift breakfast with the executive committee
6. START, STOP and KEEP team feedback

GETTING FEEDBACK

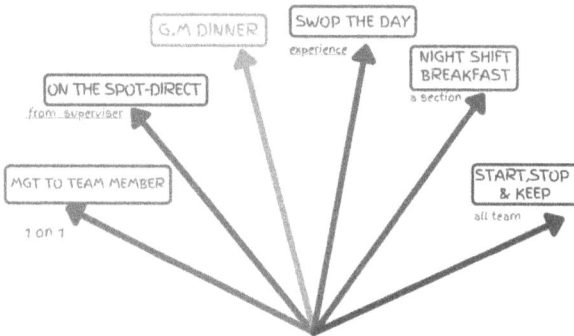

Management-to-Team Member Feedback

When we talk about feedback, we usually think of management giving feedback to a team member. What I will share with you later is the opposite - how feedback from your team could be a gift. Let's first talk about management to employee feedback - what **Monique Valcour**, an executive keynote speaker and management professor In an article published in Harvard Business Review *"How to give tough feedback that Helps people to grow"* wrote for powerful, high-impact feedback conversations, do three things:

    a.   Start with openness and humility.

b. Intend to help the employee grow, rather than to show them they were wrong.

c. Invite the employee into the problem-solving process.

The ability to give tough feedback comes up frequently. As a skills manager, I believe it is essential for leaders, but what exactly is tough feedback? The phrase connotes bad news, like when you have to tell a team member that they've screwed up on something important. Tough also signifies the way we think we need to be when giving negative feedback - firm, resolute, and unyielding.

But "tough" also points to the discomfort some of us experience when giving negative feedback. It is a challenge to motivate change, instead of making the other person feel defensive. Managers fall into a number of common traps. We might be angry at an employee and use the feedback conversation to blow off steam rather than to coach. Or we may delay giving needed feedback because we anticipate that the employee will become argumentative and refuse to accept responsibility.

We might try surrounding negative feedback with positive feedback, like a bitter tasting pill in a spoonful of honey. But this approach is misguided because we don't want the negative feedback to slip by unnoticed in the honey. Instead, it's essential to create conditions in which the receiver can take in feedback, reflect on it, and learn from it.

To get a feel for what this looks like in practice, I compared two feedback conversations that occurred following a workplace conflict. MJ Paulitz, a physical therapist in the Pacific Northwest, was treating a hospital patient one day when a fellow staff member paged her. Following a procedure, she excused herself and stepped out of the treatment room to respond to the page. The colleague who sent it didn't answer her phone when MJ called, nor had she left a message describing the situation that warranted the page.

This happened two more times during the same treatment session. The third time she left her patient to respond to the page, MJ lost her cool and left an angry voicemail message for her colleague. Upset upon hearing the message, the staff member reported it to their supervisor as abusive.

MJ's first feedback session took place in her supervisor's office. She recalls, "When I went into his office, he had already decided that I was the person at fault, he had all the information he needed, and he wasn't interested in hearing my side of the story. He did not address the three times she pulled me out of patient care. He did not acknowledge that that might have been the fuse that set me off." Her supervisor referred MJ to Human Resources for corrective action. She left seething with a sense of injustice.

MJ describes the subsequent feedback conversation with Human Resources as transformative. "The woman in HR could see that I had a lot of just-under-the-surface feelings, and she acknowledged them. The way she did it was genius: she eased into it. She didn't make me go first. Instead, she said, "I can only imagine what you're feeling right now. Here you are in my office, in corrective action. If it were me, I might be feeling angry, frustrated, embarrassed. Are any of these true for you?" That made a huge difference.

With trust established, MJ was ready to take responsibility for her behavior and commit to changing it. Next, the HR person said, "Now let's talk about how you reacted to those feelings in the moment." She created a space that opened up a genuine dialogue.

The subsequent conversation created powerful learning that has stuck with MJ to this day. "Oftentimes when we're feeling a strong emotion, we go down what the HR person called a "cowpath," because it's well worn, very narrow, and always leads to the same place.

Let's say you're angry. What do you do? You blow up. It's okay that you feel those things; it's just not okay to blow up. She asked me to think about what I could do to get on a different path."

"The feedback from the HR person helped me learn to find the space between what I'm feeling and the next thing that slides out of my mouth. She gave me the opportunity to grow internally. What made it work was establishing a safe space, trust, and rapport, and then getting down to "you need to change" rather than STARTING with "you need to change," which is what my supervisor did. I did need to change; that was the whole point of the corrective action. But she couldn't start there because I would have become defensive, shut down and not taken responsibility.

To this day, I still think that my co-worker should have been reprimanded. But I also own my part in it. I see that I went down that cowpath, and I know that I won't do it a second time.

The difference in the two feedback sessions illustrated boils down to coaching, which deepens self-awareness and catalyzes growth, versus reprimanding, which sparks self-protection and avoidance of responsibility.

To summarize, powerful, high-impact feedback conversations share the following elements:

1. Have the intention to help the employee grow, rather than to show him he was wrong. The feedback should increase, not drain, the employee's motivation and resources for change. When preparing for a feedback conversation as a manager, reflect on what you hope to achieve

and on what impact you'd like to have on the employee.

2. Openness on the part of the feedback giver is essential in creating a high-quality connection that facilitates change. If you start off feeling uncomfortable and self-protective, your employee will match that energy, and you'll each leave the conversation frustrated with the other person.

3. Invite the employee into the problem-solving process. You can ask questions such as: What ideas do you have? What are you taking away from this conversation? What steps will you take, by when, and how will I know?

Giving developmental feedback that sparks growth is a critical challenge to master because it can make the difference between an employee who contributes powerfully and positively to the organization versus one who feels diminished by the organization and contributes far less. A single conversation can switch an employee on or shut her down. A true developmental leader sees the raw material for brilliance in every employee and creates the conditions to let it shine, even when the challenge is tough.

In the previous example given by Monique Valcour, she shows that giving feedback to a team member is very important. Giving true and honest feedback is not always easy and we all too often don't value what we received from our managers, supervisors or team members enough. It is probably one of the nicest gifts they could give to us. The ability to receive tough feedback comes up as a skill essential for leaders, but what type of feedback exactly?

During my career, I always tried to be cognizant of what the team wanted. When I think about different situations, I realize I used different management styles. We are going to see different ways to get feedback that I have used throughout my career on many occasions, always with positive results for me, the team, the guests, and ultimately the business. Best of all, they are easy to implement.

On-the-Spot Direct Feedback

The first type of feedback is simply on-the-spot direct feedback from the team members that report directly to you. The first time I did it was while I was the director of Food & Beverage of a 5-star property in Phuket, Thailand.

I was working for about six months in this high-end property in Phuket, feeling for the first time in my career that I was not being totally integrated into the team and didn't know how to approach the issue. One day without really giving too much thought to it, I did something very simple that had a real positive impact with the team.

The Thai people are lovely to work with. They are hard, dedicated workers, with a great sense of service, but they don't show their emotion and it is difficult to know exactly what is on their mind. They are shy and don't like to give you feedback in front of their colleagues as they are afraid of being judged in front of their peers.

It is extremely difficult to really know what the Thai feel or think, and I needed to know how I could improve my management style and support the team better. I used to do the daily food and beverage meeting standing to make it more dynamic and quick making sure we were only covering the essentials.

In one of those meetings, I asked each team member to take a piece of paper and to write three things they wanted me to do more and three things they thought I should stop or change. I asked to have it anonymous. This was a great learning experience.

It was immediate, on-the-spot feedback from my closest team members, people who were directly reporting and working with me on a daily basis. One praise I received was that they appreciated all the training we put in place, including the incentive. So of course, I decided to continue to reinforce it.

On the other hand, I learned what not to do and got three very useful cultural suggestions I didn't even notice I was doing. One of them was that I was aggressive in my communication, even sometimes talking to guests, especially during the guest cocktail hours. I realized when I was standing and talking with guests, I often placed my hand on my hips which in the Thai culture is considered aggressive, such as a warrior ready to attack. As soon as I knew it, I stopped. To make it easier, I decided to hold a glass in my hand during the guest cocktail hour until it was over.

There were eight team members each giving me three positive feedback items and three things to improve upon. Within a month, I was able to tackle 90% of their feedback, reinforce the positive comments on purpose, and focus on correcting what they told me to improve or change.

What did I learn by doing this simple 5-minute exercise? I corrected things that my team leaders asked me to modify, but I got much more than that:

They knew I was open to their feedback, open to their ideas, suggestions, and needs.
They knew I was ready to learn from each person on the team.
I learned how to positively embrace changes.
I got a better respect of my direct team members.
I improved their trust in me.

This same exercise that I continued to do two times a year was very useful. It helped me to get better accepted by the team after a very challenging first year. I also invited them to do the same exercise with their respective teams. They all enjoyed the exercise and got some very interesting feedback as well.

How much does this cost? It's a zero investment, with only five minutes of your time, but the rewards are huge. I have of course, used this tactic a few times in different hotels and have always had a very positive outcome.

How much would you value such an exercise with your team? What would they learn about you? How much would you be ready to change? How would it impact your team? Obviously, you can't place a dollar value on it; however, you can easily understand the benefit of a mere 5-minute investment.

Weekly Feedback: Staff Dinner

Another type of feedback is having lunch or dinner with a small group of team members from different departments.

I still remember how blown away I was at the end of the evening. It was probably past 11 p.m. Our first weekly staff dinner exceeded my expectations. This was a very simple idea started by Olivier who had just joined as general manager of the hotel in South America. I was already there for two years as the executive assistant manager and I must say, this first dinner already gave us so much inside information and things to address to help the team work better and improve guest satisfaction. At that dinner, I learned how to better improve employees' working experience than I had learned in the prior two years.

The idea was simple. The GM and I were going to have a dinner with 10 staff members from different departments on a weekly basis (40 people per month). This type of activity was nothing new or revolutionary and it was happening in many hotels and organizations around the world. However, Olivier introduced a twist to those dinners. It was happening outside of work hours, (staff was picked up by the hotel and brought back home) they were able to be dress in their own clothes (no uniform), and alcohol was allowed.

Being in their own clothes, they felt more themselves and there was no distinction of departments. We learned that much of the staff had never experienced our food and never had a guest experience. The staff who were not from the food and beverage department, didn't know our menu, the atmosphere of our restaurant, and never shared a dinner with a general manager.

Dinners were very classic, nothing really special. We had a simple menu with beer or cocktail and two glasses of wine. By then, the conversation was far more interesting, and the staff members were more open and relaxed to discuss issues that were affecting them. Usually, management would bring up the topic of how we could improve guest satisfaction or how they could improve the hotel revenue and profitability.

What was interesting at those dinners was that after a few drinks, they didn't mind opening up and talking about issues that were affecting their personal life, the work organization, relations between departments, and the lack of equipment in some areas. As long as we were not solving those fundamental issues for them, guest satisfaction and increased profitability were not going to be addressed by the employee.

We focused on the staff problems, whatever they were - either knowledge of their work, training, lack of equipment, supplies, problems as simple as uniform, schedule organization, policies and procedure not well explained, etc. Most of the issues should have been solved by their supervisor or department head. The issues that were considered small details in our eyes were in fact, having a great impact on them.

The fact that we worked to solve them quickly made a great change in:

- Staff attitude and support to management.
- Helping to have a direct and more open communication between management and staff members.
- Helping us see and evaluate how Human Resources was functioning.
- How each department head was solving problems and how they were managing their teams.
- The impact on developing specific training or coaching needs for supervisors and department heads.
- Empowering staff to directly talk with the general manager which pushed department heads to have a more open, clear and truthful communication with us knowing that hiding issues was not the best option.

The estimated cost of this strategy was minimum (cost of food and wine) per month and return on investment was huge. One of the main objectives of these dinners was for the team member to relax and open up which always happened after a few glasses of beer or wine.

Not many ideas or suggestions came during the first hour, but most of the magic moments came later in the evening after they were relaxed.

Lessons learned:

- Before trying to increase revenue and profitability or improving the guest experience, the priority was to take care of the team, to improve team satisfaction.
- Give your team an opportunity to share their daily life - what they like and dislike in their job, on the team, and in the hotel.
- What was motivational for them and what was stressful for them.
- How we could help them do a better job, to improve their work life thereby improving the quality of service.
- By improving staff satisfaction, we improved our guest satisfaction.

Management Swapping Jobs for a Day

Another great way to IMPROVE your team and to learn more from them is something we did during my experience in New Orleans. Once a year for a full day, the executive team and department head would spend the entire day (lunch break included) in one department and shadow one team member. That manager would wear the same uniform as the team member he was shadowing.

Here's how it works:

Select a normal working day, not a special day that wouldn't reflect the normal operation of the department. This day was coordinated by Human Resources lead by Ray and the training manager, Monique. In one of our morning briefings a week before the swap day, Monique would draw names out of a bag. In one bag were the names of the managers and in the other bag, the names of the departments. She picked one name, then one department. You could also decide to forego the "lucky draw" and make specific arrangements by selecting a name and a department if you have a specific purpose.

We knew our executive chef Gaetan was not really communicating or at least felt like he wasn't understood by Deborah, our financial controller (FC) so we decided to have her spend a full day with Gaetan, working in the banquet kitchen.

In the eyes of our chief steward, Kevin, our maintenance manager was not spending enough time in the kitchen or taking care of the kitchen equipment, so we had constant issues with our dishwasher. Mario, the general manager was happy to spend a day at the hotel entrance as the doorman. I was lucky enough to spend the day with Marleen from the housekeeping department.

On the same day, each member of the executive committee had a day working in uniform with a team member from another department.

The day before, I passed by the laundry to pick up my new uniform and was welcomed with a big smile by Marleen who was laughing as they usually do well in New Orleans. She said, "Son, you should go to bed early tonight. Tomorrow I am going to break your back," and everyone around had a good laugh.

The next day I came on time and attended the housekeeping daily briefing and was assigned as a bellboy helper to Marleen. We had to clean 14 rooms that day - some check out rooms that required a deeper cleaning, a suite, and some regular rooms. Obviously, many of her colleagues passed by our room to check how the little "white French manager" was surviving the day.

I had a great time learning about Marleen's life, career, and issues at home, while at the same time learning all the little tricks to making a room spotless and detailed. I learned she had exceptional commitment to this difficult work, and from that day forward, we had a special bound. I still remember that day more than 20 years later. I had to do beds, clean the bathroom, and yes, she was right. At the end of eight hours of cleaning rooms, I was physically exhausted.

I learned a lot on the job but got a greater respect for all those ladies. I also realized and understood better that a change of room to please a guest was also an additional 30 minutes of work for a colleague, and from that day on when I was on duty during the weekend, I was consciously spending more time passing by the housekeeping department to see the team (that adopted me).

After that experience, as I moved to other hotels, I used to spend more time with the housekeeping department, to better understand their needs and pay more attention to their issues than if I would have not had this special day in New Orleans.

Gaetan the chef had prepared a very special day for Deborah the FC. He gave her a full kitchen experience, made sure the kitchen was hot, asked Deborah to come early and start with him at 5 a.m. so they could cook all day together. What could have happened, did happen. They had a great time working together - two strong characters gained respect for each other and they became a duet. Following that day, the executive chef started to pay more attention to Deborah's needs and recommendations, and she also gave all her support to Gaetan when he needed equipment, products, etc.

Kevin the chief engineer spent a full day in a hot, humid, busy and noisy kitchen. He paid special attention in making sure the kitchen was better supported by his department - maintenance of the exhaust hood, kitchen temperature, kitchen and equipment maintenance. He purchased some important investments that were originally postponed in the budget for a few years.

Mario our GM was the doorman. He was recognized by some of the VIP guests who complimented him for participating in that special day. He got some nice tips from the guests and enjoyed all the action, energy and good feelings the exceptional work the doorman and bell boy team were doing at the hotel entrance and in the lobby. He also better understood the valet parking issue and the exceptional work being done by the concierge and front office in accommodating guests' often last-minute special requests.

Lessons learned:

- There are things you can only learn by doing it. Spending eight hours in a different and challenging work environment with team members was a really nice and useful learning day. It provided us with a better understanding that led us to more support and more empathy. That day spent was a great success.

- Each executive had very positive feedback, more energy, and everyone was happy to be back in his department with a sense of gratitude and empathy for their colleague and respect for their work. This is a great exercise that required a little bit of preparation and coordination with absolutely no additional cost.

Once you have a better understanding of other departments, team members, and challenges they face, you may desire to support and help them. From my experience and feedback from other executive members, this has helped us to better understand the challenges and difficulty faced by the rank-and-file work.

Night Shift Breakfast with the Executive Committee

If you lead a rather large operation you can also invite an area that you don't meet with often. When I was in Islamabad, Pakistan and worked for The Serena hotel chain that belongs to Prince Agha Khan, we wanted to get direct feedback from the team. That was pretty easy to put in place for most of the teams, however we couldn't get with the large night shift team who worked 11 p.m. to 7 a.m.

Working at night, team members were more disconnected and not always aware of changes or new processes. This was a great tool once a month for HR and the executive team to engage a direct dialogue with them. We decided that once a month, we would have a beautiful breakfast with the entire night shift team, approximately fifty people in one of our banquet rooms with the same setup as our guests.

After the first two to three meetings, the employees were asking for some minor changes and had easy requests. I realized that all their concerns were focused on the guests and the security of everyone within the hotel. Indeed, at that time, security was one of the main problems we were facing. When employees' ideas, suggestions, and proposals focus on the guests, it is a very positive sign. It says that their needs were satisfied and they were happy and motivated. We knew the team was doing good work to keep the staff motivated.

START, STOP, and KEEP Team Feedback

I discovered this type of feedback not when I was in the hospitality industry, but while I was coach. I used this type in many businesses with great results. Why do I use this strategy? It's a nice way to get thematic ideas and feedback directly from the team.

Once I was in a coaching session with a guest. He was complaining about the lack of creativity, ideas and suggestions from his team. Instead of doing the following week's sessions, I asked Peter if I could have all the team members available for a one-hour meeting with me. I asked him to get five poster boards, some post-its (sticker paper) and send me four or five subjects he would like to get feedback on and ideas from his team. The following week Peter and his team were ready for the activity "Start, Stop and Keep" team feedback.

Why do it? I was doing a session with Peter, the owner of the business, and he was complaining that he had to bring all the ideas to the table. His team was not creative, they had very few suggestions on how to increase revenue, how to improve teamwork, or how to increase guest satisfaction. He was somehow telling me he had to do everything.

I learned this from one of the greatest business coaches, Andrew Johnson, from ActionCOACH based in New Zealand. Here's how it works:

Decide four or five topics that you want to have feedback on from your team (employee satisfaction, guest experience, sales and marketing, finance, operations) or a specific issue you have in your operation that you want to improve on. Place each topic on a large poster board divided in three columns. Write on the top of the first column START, on the second column STOP, and on the third column KEEP. Divide your team into groups of two to four people. Each group stays in front of one poster board. Give each participant some post-its and a pen and ask them to write on their post-it note one idea and place it either on the START, the STOP or the KEEP column. They can write as many ideas as they want. When you see that many have finished (approximately five minutes per poster board) ask each group to rotate clockwise to the next poster board until each team member has been able to give their feedback on each topic.

The second step is to count each column's total number of stickers (1 sticker = 1 idea). Add the three columns together and you have the total number of ideas per poster board. Add the numbers of ideas of all your poster boards - easily 100?

Peter couldn't believe his staff could come up with so many great ideas in less than 30 minutes, without spending a lot of time and effort. Of course, some ideas were double. However, it was impressive, and everyone had great energy.

The second phase was to review each poster board and classify ideas in three categories A, B and C.

A are ideas that are easy to implement, require no time and no budget. For example, let's start a monthly problem-solving meeting.

B ideas are the ones that are important but require some time to analyze - to get some data, check the cost, need some planning or might require outside authorization before implementation, i.e., start a Sunday brunch with entertainment, do a Thai food promotion, get new guest welcome amenities.

C ideas might be very interesting; however, they are not in your 3-year vision or 12-month goals. They would require time for further study. Analysis might involve a large cost, a budget approval from the owner, etc. i.e., let's have a new guest market and build a spa.

A idea will be put into action in the next 90 days, B ideas would be included in your 12-month goals, C ideas might be placed in the following year.

START column: These are the most interesting as they might bring a lot of positivity and energy to the team.

STOP column: Check with the team. If you get agreement from the team, act immediately. Test and measure for 90 days and evaluate the effects. Don't underestimate the positive impact of stopping something that annoys the majority of the team. Does that affect your guests? Your suppliers?

KEEP column: It is nice for you to know what your team likes and wants for the business to continue. You could also try to work on those ideas if you feel there is a room for improvement.

Peter had a paradigm shift. He thought his team was not interested and he realized with this exercise that the team was just waiting for an opportunity to be listened to. We selected three ideas from each poster board to put in place within the next 90 days, 15 in all. Peter was happy and more aware of what his team liked in the way he was running his business.

What do you think happened? Peter never complained to me about the lack of creativity of his team. New ideas brought a new spirit and teamwork, members felt listened to, and felt better understood and empowered. The team was felt empowered and overall results improved. Nothing should stop you from doing this exercise once a year. This exercise is simple and cheap.

There are many other ways to get valuable feedback from your team and I am sure you already have some strategies or will learn more over the months and years to come. Start to implement those six simple non-costly exercises to IMPROVE your team, then share with me your results.

Your Strategy #7 Action:

- Plan those six ways over the next six months to get feedback from your team.
- Start direct, on-the-spot feedback within the next seven days.
- Organize a "start, stop, and keep" activity in the next 30 days.
- Next month, select a small group of 6 to 10 people from your organization to have lunch or dinner with.
- In the next 90 days, plan a swap-the-day with the kitchen, stewarding, reception, housekeeping, etc.
- Note for each what you have learned from your team. What have you been able to change from this?
- Don't stop being creative and finding new ways of getting feedback from your team.

Chapter Ten

STRATEGY #8
LEADERSHIP QUESTIONS

The Seven Questions for Better Leadership

Another strategy to IMPROVE your team is to have a system that will keep you constantly aligned with your direct reports providing feedback, coaching and recognition.

The Seven-Question Process

Why would you use these seven questions of leadership?

I learned this process from Marshall Goldsmith, considered to be one of the best executive coaches in the world. He has used it with major CEOs around the world with great success. He found that often leaders spend less time with their managers but are more structured, have more direction and more clarity, and their time was used in a much better way.

What is the seven-question process? Every two to three months you sit with your direct report and have a one-on-one dialogue to discuss six basic issues.

QUESTIONS BETTER LEADERSHIP

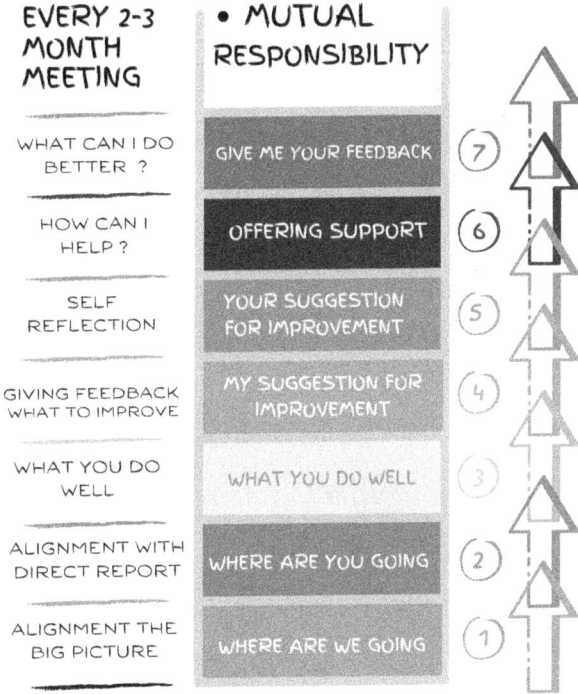

EVERY 2-3 MONTH MEETING	• MUTUAL RESPONSIBILITY	
WHAT CAN I DO BETTER ?	GIVE ME YOUR FEEDBACK	7
HOW CAN I HELP ?	OFFERING SUPPORT	6
SELF REFLECTION	YOUR SUGGESTION FOR IMPROVEMENT	5
GIVING FEEDBACK WHAT TO IMPROVE	MY SUGGESTION FOR IMPROVEMENT	4
WHAT YOU DO WELL	WHAT YOU DO WELL	3
ALIGNMENT WITH DIRECT REPORT	WHERE ARE YOU GOING	2
ALIGNMENT THE BIG PICTURE	WHERE ARE WE GOING	1

Question 1: Where are we going?

Have a dialogue. "As your manager this is how I see the business, the organization going." and ask, "How do you see the business going?" This is a 2-way communication. "Here is where I see we should be going. Where do YOU think we should be going?"

Question 2: - Where are YOU Going?

Get in alignment with your direct report. The first question was on the big picture about the business. The second is more focused on the person and his department. "This is where I see you and your part of the business going. Where do you see yourself going?"

Question 3: What Do You Think You Are Doing Well?

This is a question we don't ask leadership enough. "As your leader, this is what I see you and your department doing well. What do you think you are doing well? What are you proud of? You can learn a lot from this question and discover something noteworthy that has been done but you have not paid enough attention to it. As a manager, it is a good time to recognize you realized and appreciated the effort your manager did.

Question 4: What are Some Suggestions for Improvement?

"As your manager, here are some suggestions for improvement that might help you to do even better moving forward." Feed forward (no feedback in the past) - give ideas that might help for the future.

Question 5: Self-Reflection - What Are Your Suggestions for Improvement?

"If you were your coach, what advice or ideas would you have for yourself for improvement?" As you listen, you will be shocked at what you are going to learn.

One of my friends Sophie that has additional responsibility for the CEO's union at the regional and national level didn't know how to organize her life. In the meantime, she was running her own business. She was struggling to see how she could reorganize her life. When she asked this question to a key member of her team, she realized that he wanted to move up in the company and have more responsibility.

The solution was right in front of her, but she didn't notice it. You might also often find that their ideas are better than your ideas for improvement, so in this case, go with their ideas first.

Question 6: Am I Offering Support?

"As a leader how can I help you? We've talked about what you want to do and where you want to go as a leader. How can I help you to get there?"

Question 7: What Suggestion do You Have for Me to Be a Better Manager?

"How can I be more effective as your manager?" This a 2-way dialogue. You are both trying to help each other.

The key to the success of this dialogue process is the mutual responsibility. You need to say, "Once every two to three months I am going to go through these seven basic issues with you. If at any time you feel a sense of ambiguity, confusion on priority, or you're un-clear on the direction of something, I want you to tell me if you need more feedback or coaching. You need to take responsibility. If I take responsibility to do my job in covering those seven basic questions every two to three months, and you take responsibility in between time, there is absolutely no reason we should have any doubt or confusion in terms of clarity, direction, coaching, or feedback."

As a leader, if you want to do a better job in providing clarity, coaching, feedback, or recognition, the seven-question process can help you get there.

Your Strategy #8 Action:

- Implement the seven questions for better leadership with your direct reports.

Chapter Eleven

STRATEGY #9 A PRACTICAL ACTION PLAN

Using the Skills-Enjoyment Matrix

As the leader of your winning team, the way you invest your time is critical. You might think at the end of this book, "With all the new things I need to do or start implementing, I am never going to have time." So in a few weeks you will have not taken any action and ultimately, I will have wasted your time. This last exercise is going to help you to focus on what you want and need to do for the business.

It is important. You are probably the most important or the highest-paid person on the team, so you better make sure the time spent in your business is wisely invested. You can use a very simple matrix with two axes - one would be the activities, tasks and required skills and the second would be the activity that you enjoy doing or that gives you the most energy.

By doing this exercise you will get clarity on which activities you need to focus on in your business and with your team, what you need to delegate, and what will get more positive energy as you will be spending more time on activities you like to do and became more productive.

On the matrix select the 10 to 15 activities that require most of your time during the week/month. Plot all the tasks you do in the matrix according to the level of skill required to do the task and the level of enjoyment you get from doing it. Horizontally, the more you go to your right, the more you enjoy doing those activities.

And the more you go vertically from the top down, those activities require high skills. What do you think you should prioritize?

STRATEGY #9

SKILL . PLEASURE . MATRIX

YOUR	**ZONE**	Y O U
DELEGATION	IF POSSIBLE	R Z O
D E L E G A T I O N		N E

SKILL

PLEASURE

Your Strategy # 9 Action

1. Implement your seven questions of leadership with your direct reports.
2. Do your skills – fun matrix.
3. Prioritize your time according to skills and pleasure.
4. Coach your leader to do the same.

As a quick reminder here are the nine strategies to BUILD, GROW, and IMPROVE your team.

3 strategies to BUILD your team

- Your 1-page plan including 3-year vision, 12-month goal and a 90-day plan.
- Who is on your team? Use the performance and value matrix.
- Recruitment using two types of interviews and the 25 questions to select your next team members.

3 strategies to GROW your team

- Coach your key team members.
- Use four types of communications.
- All problems should **be** solved by the leader in charge.

3 strategies to IMPROVE your team

- Receiving feedback is a gift.
- Seven questions for better leadership.
- Where do you need to be using the skills
  – enjoyment matrix.

Act tomorrow and start implementing these nine strategies in your next 90-day goals, then test and measure your results. Adjust and adapt them to your needs.

Finally

CONCLUSION

To conclude, I would like to share a short story that I read a few years ago. When I think about a team I would love to lead, I always think about Ubuntu. This word/concept comes from the Xhosa culture in South Africa.

One day an anthropologist did an experiment with kids. He placed them on the same line and told them they would have to run to the tree furthest away. The first one to reach the tree will be able to enjoy a large basket full of delicious fresh fruit. He gave them the departure signal and was very surprised by what he saw. No one raced. All the children decided to hold each other's hands, walk together to the tree and share the delicious fruits together. He was surprised at the lack of competition. He asked the children why they did that. They explained, "How can we each be happy if the others are sad." That is the philosophy you want to develop in your business, the concept of winning together.

The stories I have shared with you to illustrate the nine strategies will help you have a happier team who is willing to win together. I hope you have found some useful strategies and will implement them in your business. If not all of them, at least some to BUILD, GROW and IMPROVE your team. I wish you fun and much success.

If you wish to receive more information you can send an email to guillaumewarnery@hotel-coach.pro or visit

Guillaume is available for Speaking engagements either live or via Video (Zoom), workshops, Interviews and retreats.

His current Speaking topics are as follows

1. What category 5 Hurricane Wilma has taught me about leading teams in crisis and recovery.

2. From small rainforest lodges to large resort & spa, from city hotel to Leading Hotels of the World, what I have learned in increasing profitability and leading happy teams

3. Leading people in 10 countries over five continents have helped me to understand the power of feedback in 4 ways in order to connect, engage & boost teams .

4. Inspiring teams through terrorist threat, economic crisis , natural disaster, change of ownership and dealing with strong staff unions